Dear Meister,

May you always remember that we're all born with an "inner sparkle" — that spills over into anyone's life that we take the time to touch!

Thanks also for being one of my Biggest cheerleaders!!

Good luck with those knees!

Love ya,
"Spike"

# S.P.A.R.K.L.E.

## Nancy Loss

Copyright © 2014 by Nancy Loss.

All rights reserved. No part of this book may be used or reproduced by any means, graphic, electronic, or mechanical, including photocopying, recording, taping or by any information storage retrieval system without the written permission of the publisher except in the case of brief quotations embodied in critical articles and reviews.

Cover design by Robert Scalzo, Striking Poses Portrait Studio (strikingposesportraitstudio.com).

Nancy Loss' photograph taken by Robert Scalzo.

Cover image (painting of angel) by artist, Esther Mason.

Scripture taken from the New King James Version ®.
Copyright ©1982 Thomas Nelson Inc.
Used by permission. All rights reserved.

*** A portion of the proceeds from the sale of this book will be donated to: The Seeing Eye, Inc. which is the oldest existing guide dog school in the world, aiding those affected by blindness to become all they were born to be!

WestBow Press books may be ordered through booksellers or by contacting:

WestBow Press
A Division of Thomas Nelson & Zondervan
1663 Liberty Drive
Bloomington, IN 47403
www.westbowpress.com
1 (866) 928-1240

Because of the dynamic nature of the Internet, any web addresses or links contained in this book may have changed since publication and may no longer be valid. The views expressed in this work are solely those of the author and do not necessarily reflect the views of the publisher, and the publisher hereby disclaims any responsibility for them.

ISBN: 978-1-4908-2793-3 (sc)
ISBN: 978-1-4908-2792-6 (hc)
ISBN: 978-1-4908-2794-0 (e)

Library of Congress Control Number: 2014903859

Printed in the United States of America.

WestBow Press rev. date: 05/02/2014

# CONTENTS

Dedication .................................................................................. vii
Acknowledgements ..................................................................... ix
Preface ...................................................................................... xiii
Introduction ............................................................................... xv

My Personal Wish for You .............................................................. 1
How My "S.P.A.R.K.L.E. Theory" Started ........................................ 3
What Would Be in Your "Do-It-in-Ninety-Days" Duffel Bag? ......... 7
When "Mrs. Sawyer" Suddenly Needed Me ................................. 13
A Simply Spectacular Story .......................................................... 17
The Best Buck I Ever Spent .......................................................... 21
Thank God for Stretch Marks ....................................................... 23
Trading Control for Carefree ....................................................... 33
As One Door Opens, Another Closes - ....................................... 37
Taking Time Out for Guaranteed Giggles - ................................. 43
Living Life as Lovable ................................................................. 49
Fate Doesn't Forget ..................................................................... 51
Answers Always from my Favorite Author .................................. 61
From Fearful to Fruitful – While Learning to Laugh Again .......... 75
The Day I Drove that Scary Bridge .............................................. 81
When "The Angel" Ended Up Being Me ..................................... 83
In Loving Memory of Michael Steven Torres, USMC ................... 93
Yet "Another Michael's" Magic .................................................... 97
My Biggest Pet Peeve ................................................................ 101

A True Inspiration to All ................................................................. 105
I Know What It's Like ................................................................... 115
The Day the Gosling Got Let Go .................................................. 121
Whose Life Have You Left Imprints On? ..................................... 125
Each of us has a dream… ............................................................. 127
Some Real Support of Steel ......................................................... 129
Your Birthday should be Beautiful – ........................................... 135
Because We Are Never Too Old For Surprises! ........................... 149

About the Author .......................................................................... 153
And Now, For the Real Icing on the Cake… ................................ 155
The Best is yet to Come! .............................................................. 157
Suggested Reading for "Real Sparklers" ..................................... 161

# DEDICATION

This book is dedicated to everyone who believes that people cross our paths for a reason. And, that behind every stressful situation remains the option to stress less. As blissfully, when our lives are being overshadowed with "all that we aren't in the eyes of others" – maybe we are meant to rest and reflect more in the Lord's love and pursue our brightest light?

Moreover, for my cherished readers, I hope that you'll find within these sacredly-penned pages some uplifting inspiration from my own "Seven Special Sparklers" – whose challenging journeys weren't always easy, yet with a heartfelt mix of mirrored friendship, "family" and forgiveness have sweetly managed to come out on top!

> "Each one of us is created with an inherent light within. A light made up of limitless spiritual power. It's solely up to you to determine how brightly you let your light shine and whether or not you allow the world to rejoice in the rays of its healing glow.
> ~ Oprah Winfrey

# ACKNOWLEDGEMENTS

"Every great dream begins with a dreamer. Always remember, you have within you the strength, the patience, and the passion to reach for the stars to change the world."

~ Harriet Tubman

With special thanks to Dr. Michael Torres, as it was many years ago as I was multitasking like a dingy amidst being "Wonder Mom" daily, while also painfully watching my ailing grandfather, Poppy, begin to seriously go downhill – that I just simply blurted out one day: "What do you do when everything you are doing in life, is ALWAYS never enough?" Where at this point I was truly expecting a little dose of sympathy, but instead, as "Doc" next slurped a bit more of his lukewarm coffee he just answered me back very quickly. Where wondrously too, while shrugging his shoulders as he walked out the door, he enlightened this so, at-times wilderness lady with the words of just "Do less." Yet, here also, while others would try and speculate about the real facts behind our friendship, it would somehow be this never-thought-of-before concept, that would not only become a treasured mantra in my life, but has solidly been one of the stepping stones I've needed to timely complete this second book. After all, both Dr. Torres and I were learning as well, to let the Lord control our worlds as now willfully practicing (but wobbly!) Christians - in everything from parenthood to paychecks to even humbly picking our life's partner. Though, while also discussing as well, that total surrender can be scary, we knew there was no way that God would be able to use us amid His Grace-filled insights if we did not let Him in!

Next, I would also like to thank my Patient Access Supervisor, Darlene Benten, for unknowingly providing me with every personal day she could juggle in the last few months, so I could devote more of my freed-up time to completing this much-cherished walk. With love also to my special friend, Sherry Falcone-Struminski, for not only repeating regularly to me: "Don't Let Anyone Steal Your SPARKLE," but for always treating me regardless of my strides or stumbles, like the sister that you've never had. Furthermore, I would like to thank my mirroring friend since middle school, Julie Zito-Clark, for always believing as I do, that between "both refusing to sell our hearts out and those matching looks on our faces when we would regularly just rush by each other at the mall" that we're all meant for something more. That is, only wholeheartedly, if we have the gumption to go for it. Therefore, after recently receiving your awesome message with no-holds-barred of, "I have reached my moment" - though you will be truly missed, I know, that when it comes to any of my friend's surely God-guided missions I have never been more proud!

At this time also, I would like to acknowledge my handful of "Heaven sent angels" - who unconditionally provide both their energy and expertise always at the drop of a hat. Likewise, a major thanks goes out to Robert Scalzo, my photographer and (very purple!) cover designer and to Esther Mason, for her artistic talent that has so-steadfastly painted that sweet angel we'd both envisioned, whose sparkling charisma and serene comfort now grace this treasured book. Kudos also, to Beth Mac Swan, Donna Crow, "T-Bear" and Brenda Wellar – as without their dedicated copying, computer and correcting finesse, this work would still be a dream! Moreover, to all my heroes and heroines along for this next enlightening endeavor (most of whom on this joyful journey, have first names consisting only of five letters), amidst always making me feel just like I "fit" and that I'm family, I will always cherish your faith and support. Furthermore, I truly am indebted to my Seven Special Sparklers, whose stories highlight these illuminating pages, as it's their impact and inspiration that surely kept me late-night typing, even as my hands did throb. Moreover, for everyone who has repeatedly asked why my first book's cover wasn't created in some really stellar shade of purple - I hope this second's release makes you smile, because this one's for you!

Yet, lastly once again remains my gratitude to God first and foremost, for allowing me, not only to learn to "Do Less" but to continually remain awestruck - as I too, read on channeled paper what His never-ending belief in my awakened destiny, delightfully allows my body to do!

"There is no passion to be found in settling for a life that is less than the one you are capable of living."
~ Nelson Mandela

# PREFACE

It has been a little over a year ago, since my first book *Life Is How YOU Look At It* launched. Though, what some of you may not know is that this miracle-filled experience contained enough life lessons and light bulb moments to fill at least two more treasured works. Yet, it is now this bigger picture's awareness that has me hunkering down in obedience to fulfill a promise that I've primarily made to God. You see, a few years ago when my gift of writing truly withered, I begged the Lord that "if He brought it back to blossoming," I would not let him down. Also, as part of this publishing endeavor's pathway, I was told explicitly as I prayerfully listened, that there would be a total of three of His wisdom-laced books. Of which, dear readers, this spiritual illumination amongst surely divine intervention was the easiest part. As the other piece of fulfilling the Lord's exact specifications (amidst being a woman still working two jobs), was knowing that I would need to willfully slow down more and savor my energy - to both accomplish this very tall order as I had promised, and within His given timeframe of only five years. All this, while dodging an onslaught of ugliness aimed daily at me, "of all that I supposedly wasn't in my travels" to be able to pull this predestined task off! Where finally, could it be that for all of those times where others keep trying to magnify our "shortcomings," that we are expected to S.P. A.R.K.L.E. the most?

> "Your value doesn't decrease on someone's inability to see your worth."
> 
> ~ Unknown

# INTRODUCTION

There's so much I'm still learning after successfully publishing my first book, *Life Is How YOU Look At It*, and would like to share a few things that continue to top the list. First off, I am a true believer in God's Sacred Timing, as whenever I'd get antsy about wanting to know my original book's release date – all the Lord, would share with me is that: "It would all make sense in the end." Meanwhile, every time I would try to (still so-humorously now) hurry along the process, I'd get another life lesson to learn! For example, in order to try and have the necessary funds upfront to publish I next raided my small retirement plan about four years ago. Yet, only to find that once I did, the same twelve hundred dollars I had received was suddenly needed, for my Grad School daughter's unexpected dental surgery for that exact amount. In also being able to hear from God I've found, that the more I chose to ignore His Wisdom that the louder He would get. Therefore, if truth be told, while my manifested manuscript did surreally publish – it truly DID make sense in the end! You see, during mid-September of 2012, my hardcover edition released on my late childhood best friend's birthday – where we had been pals since about the age of four, when she died tragically in a car accident and headed home to heaven at the young age of twenty one. Next, my softcover copy landed in my mailbox on none other than my nineteenth anniversary of proudly working in the Emergency Room Registration area at Mount St. Mary's Hospital. Then, by sweetly managing to publish by some still-unknown-to-me deadline, I was wondrously represented in the biggest book show in the country in Orlando, Florida- on none-other-than my birthday, November eighteenth as well! All this ultimately, with only five bucks in one bank account and three dollars in another, while leading me to forever believe, that if things are meant to happen hope will always find a way.

Meanwhile it still never ceases to amaze me how God continues to send me both the talent and tales of others to help me to fill these promised pages. Especially in a way He knows that I would understand- and, even without my late Poppy's presence or the reassurance of his precious red roses placed lovingly into my hands. As such would be the case most recently, when I needed an unexpected adjustment at my chiropractor's office. Likewise, it was here, that I'd run into an old friend named "Esther," (which is also one of my most cherished nicknames after being told that my long, flannel old-lady nightgown collection resembles those of "Grandma Walton") - would instantly make this comfort-quilt encounter one, where my ears would really perk up! Where, next, this kind-hearted woman would begin to ask me about the status of my first book. Then, I'd share with her how I was so very close to completing the second, but also struggling to find an artist amidst praying ever-diligently, for someone who'd be able to paint a special angel for the front of my S.P.A.R.K.L.E.-themed book. Where at this time, sweet Esther would enlighten me here, that even amongst her two College degrees how she is actually also an artist, and then invited me to both stop by for a visit and be able to view her work. Therefore, upon my arrival you can imagine my surprise, when she kept "such a truly stellar collection of some previously pencil sketched angels" stored right behind her couch! Furthermore it is my hope that as you read these treasured pages filled with both real pain and refreshing positives, I encourage you to focus less on my writing style as it's not always grammatically perfect but largely how I "hear it" – and more about the blissful promise of with Our Father's help, being all that you can be! Here, please also note: While some people's names and stories contained herein, have been changed for their protection of privacy - it has remained one of my biggest goals in this tapestry-tied work (that's not always in order again by timeline), to keep their sparkle intact.

"I believe that life is given us so that we may grow in love, and I believe that God is in me as the sun is in the color and fragrance of a flower – the Light in my darkness, the Voice in my silence."

~ Helen Keller

# MY PERSONAL WISH FOR YOU

May Your Priorities In Life Be Focused On …

Abundance instead of Anger
Blessings instead of Berating
Creativity instead of Criticism
Desires instead of Deprivation
Energy instead of Exhaustion
Forgiveness instead of Failure
Growth Spurts instead of Guilt
Happiness instead of Humiliation
Inner Peace instead of Irony
Just Being instead of Judgment
Kindness instead of Chaos
Laughter instead of Loneliness
Miracles instead of Mourning
New Horizons instead of Negativity
Opportunities instead of Oversights
Passion instead of Powerlessness
Quiet Times instead of Craziness
Rebirth instead of Regret
Serenity instead of "Shoulds"
Tender Touches instead of Temper Outbursts
Understanding instead of Unfulfilling
Victories instead of Vulnerability
Wholeness instead of Wishing
And, Youthfulness instead of Yearning
With a "Zest for Life" From God Above
Forever Wrapped in Grateful Love!

ENJOY!
In peace and prayers…
Love,
Nancy

> "We are each gifted in a unique and important way. It is our privilege and our adventure to discover our own special light."
>
> ~ Mary Dunbar

# HOW MY "S.P.A.R.K.L.E. THEORY" STARTED

About six months ago, I was listening as always, to our local Christian Radio Station, on the way home from work. Where here also, as it was raining like crazy, the special hosts were inviting any willing listeners to please call in and share what strategies and secrets truly held us together during the toughest of times in our lives. They also wanted to know what works for us best "when we talk to ourselves" during stress. In the meantime, once home amidst being totally drenched and still shivering, I sat down quickly at the computer desk and began to rapidly scribble some thoughts. Then, as no stranger to Satan's sabotage, I found the phone line to be repeatedly busy, even as I redialed with palpitations and kept holding my breath with hope. Next, my tiny dog, Bandit, began an unusually long, snorting fit of his surely reverse sneezing - that to my delight seemed to dissipate just as a male's voice next picked up. And, while nothing would be more comforting to me, then to learn his name was "Michael" – since I mindfully knew, that this name like that of my guardian angel's brings me only the best of luck. While we next reviewed my list of what I hoped to share across the WDCX airwaves, Michael inquisitively asked at this time, where I had actually learned all of this treasured information from. Where humbly here, I now relayed to him, that I "not only lived right in their broadcasting backyard" – but had also been on a wondrously God-guided journey, that resulted in writing a book. Meanwhile, as we next discussed how it would not be allowed on my part to simply promote my newly-published work Michael said he "would only let me mention my manuscript," if these two hosts should ask about the history of my healing, somehow optimally here head-on. At this point also, I am thrilled to say, that the Lord once again parted His Red Sea of promise, to see that my purpose propelled along. After all, while being questioned here and awesomely on the air amid a two-way conversation, I tried-and-true mentioned, that under all the hailstorms and heartaches I'd been through, I learned there was always hope. Moreover, I added positively that, "If God prunes you for your higher purpose He provides both the rock and the roadmap as well." At this juncture too, both hosts fell silent as listening intently, then Neil Boron inquisitively asked me, how I basically "knew what I knew." Now for me, this answer came easy, as my nerves next rapidly dissipated while being able to enlighten all others within earshot - about my *Life Is How YOU Look At It's* legacy, and so loving to do God's work! (Remarkably too, it had only been a few days earlier that I was reflecting back over my first book's journey out on my sun-drenched lawn swing, and pondering that which I wished my readers would remember from it most. When, it was at this light bulb moment, that I hoped they would recall especially from my Helen Keller's tribute - that we are all born with an "inner sparkle" that spills over into anyone's life that we take the time to touch. Likewise, it was also here on this truly soggy morning, that my S.P.A.R.K.L.E. theory was revisited while meditating on my lunch break, amongst surely becoming the set-in-stone theme for this second blessing-filled book!)

  Then, while finishing up on the air on that rainy day with both Neil and his special guest, Carol McLeod, I shared amongst the audience, how two comforting thoughts always keep me foremost solid when any of life's turbulence or tragedies hit. Besides, if truth be told, we can't always control what happens around us but we *can* control how we react! Therefore, I stated finally also, that from my cherished Reverend, Father Noah, I'd forever-grasped amid true gratefulness, that "No matter what I am going through, I should always Focus on Up." Moreover, during those times that I encounter that are both really tough and tender, I tell myself religiously that I have the choice to S.P.A.R.K.L.E.– that is, amidst rebuking other's chronic negativity, consciously begin the awesome journey to:

<u>S</u>eriously

<u>P</u>ursue

<u>A</u>

<u>R</u>elationship (with the)

<u>K</u>ing of

<u>L</u>ife

<u>E</u>verlasting – and let Him take over the reins!

*** Since excitedly now, I above-all know, that even as this never-expected-to-be author has been so-graciously enabled again to publish, that I NEVER go anywhere alone! Delightfully also, in this miracle-filled expedition, God continues to have both my back and my best interests- as He lovingly nurtures my instilled gifts just like those of my late Grammie, as I'd excitedly watched while her so-cherished ceramic pieces went from the mold stage to a masterpiece.

> "One of the biggest things in my life is that I've been able to connect with thousands of people heart to heart. The world needs what only you were divinely created to share."
>
> ~ Oprah Winfrey

Meet "Bandit" my five-year-old Poodle, who if he isn't busy keeping my feet warm as I write at the computer, simply steals my pillow instead!

# WHAT WOULD BE IN YOUR "DO-IT-IN-NINETY-DAYS" DUFFEL BAG?

> "Come to Me, all you who labor and are heavy laden, and I will give you rest. Take My yoke upon you and learn from Me, for I am gentle and lowly in heart, and you will find rest for your souls."
>
> Matthew 11: 28, 29
> "NKJV™"

Okay, I admit it, I've been slacking. Although, I'd promised the Lord to produce three total books in willfully five years, the woeful bigger picture has since revealed, that I was too busy to even sit still. Furthermore, while it would be easiest to blame my distracted desire to manifest another manuscript on everything like the deer-hit, the heightened drama, and our dog's repeated illnesses – the real fact remained that in order to harvest another proposed book by the end of this year, I would need to both hunker down and clean out my personal clutter just to be able to hear more from God. Meanwhile, this epiphany occurred on August 18, 2013. This date was also just a few days before my cherished Poppy had sadly now died, almost thirteen years ago. To my surprise too, this moment was surreally as well, ninety days exactly to the date of my upcoming fiftieth birthday. When, suddenly here I realized, that since "most of the grief in my heart had surely been sacredly lifted," I just might be able to pull this task off! Also, in my heart I knew, what this effort was going to entail. After all, I'd learned amid completing my first book, that if I didn't keep Jesus' wisdom first and foremost in my life, my world would just keep falling apart. Besides, while this spiritual slowdown wasn't going to make for some real happy campers from within my inner circle, the real reality shone ever-so-brightly that: while some others remained largely busy addressing their "fan club's needs"

– whether around or helping others, I'd been pretty much left on my own.

Though, it would be at this point also, that I would willfully review as well, from *Life Is How YOU Look At It,* all those faithful strategies that had previously worked wonders for me. Where, before I knew it, I would be fasting for most meals, walking so-nature-filled Niagara Falls and finding the necessary time to nap again - to optimally arise in the overnights to hear what the Lord wanted me to write. At the same time, I was cutting down on working overtime, spending less energy on the internet, and would now only do a cycle of errands on my way home from work. Here too, it occurred to me as well: "Wouldn't it be wonderful if our own wilted relationships were given as much positive attention, like we attempt to portray on our public pages?" Yet more than anything I'd revealed from this book-birthing insight that, "If God wills you for your Higher Purpose, He provides both the means and the miracles as well." But, I also found that this pruning process can be really painful, as not only does it strip us down to our most vulnerable of sensibilities, but shows us majorly also, what we can really do without. Finally, from reflecting further upon my previous book's journey, I was so blissfully reminded, that whenever some (once-thought, sparse) flickers of sabotaging turbulence began to escalate ten-fold, that: "We are all survivors of something" but still standing is no SMALL thing!

One day, amidst this surely can-do attitude, I found myself eagerly beginning to clean out my mailboxes at work. At the same time, just by spotting a coworker's now half-slurped cup of coffee basically sitting on our office's back counter – it suddenly took my mind back to that illuminating day when Dr. Mike Torres amongst my discussing the stress of my avalanched life load, - simply suggested that I learn to "Do less." When humorously as well, this cherished tapestry thread's recollection, next divinely began the process to "consciously fill a medium-sized duffel bag with the necessary tools needed" to hopefully go from nurtured manuscript-to-mission pre-printed, in now under ninety days! Here also, I would sweetly uncover a small, white book that I'd always promised myself to read within my THREE truly overstuffed mailboxes' contents, from fruit snacks to folders, memos to markers and some highlighters to hair clips to boot. Then, by simply picking up Martha Beck's book, *The Joy Diet- 10 Daily Practices For A Happier Life*, I felt a surge of warmth shoot right through my solar plexus – so boldly letting me know, that there was something within its very beckoning contents that I was totally meant to learn! Therefore, begin reading I did, as its worthwhile words would unveil to me the nurturing benefits of "actually doing nothing" for at least fifteen minutes a day, while also delightfully putting our fingers on those once-only-underlying-wishes that may propel us towards our dreams. Moreover, as Martha's story continues, she also opens up about how, after some major bouts of exhaustion amid many health-related crises, mixed also with having a disabled child – sweetly here, some healing avenues also appeared, that would begin to teach her the therapeutic benefits of mindfully slowing down. Likewise, to further enhance our own skills on the subject of "doing nothing" she advises that the following self-nurturing strategy should ultimately begin today:

"Right now schedule at least fifteen minutes every day (twenty, if you can get it) for nothing-doing. Then, each day at the appointed time, go to any comfortable, quiet spot. ... For this short time, you must be absolutely unavailable and inaccessible to *everyone*. Let it be known that you are fully occupied, that you have no room for anyone until you have finished doing nothing. Do whatever it takes to light up the NO VACANCY sign in your life."

Meanwhile, my cherished duffel bag would contain a few more special items - such as my favorite blanket to rest upon, when I wrote down at the sun-filled falls. Here too, I would regularly rotate amongst the revealing "Joyce Meyer" books I'd been rereading, where one would so assertively teach me over time that: "I have the right to experience joy in any situation that I'm in." So here, like many other spiritually-sensitive people (even as some obvious critics relentlessly tried "to hang their hats on all I supposedly wasn't, when they, themselves, were called out on the carpet"), I chose to be less affected by any childish antics and just continued to hold my head high. But, more than anything I knew, from both my elementary school assignments amongst two very educated parents, that if I just hurriedly threw something together that didn't sparkle within this divinely-led endeavor, both my much loved "family" and the Lord would notice, and then just like when I was younger I'd be hanging around home 'til it did.

At the same time, I would rely on Doreen Virtue's book, *Divine Guidance – How to Have a Dialogue with God and Your Guardian Angels'* enlightenment once again, to keep my trek on track. Moreover, she would state some facts about how "those divine interventions like visions, smells and voices" – are truly some ways that we may communicate with God's wisdom or His very soothing angels as well. Where here also, she would shed more light on those feelings of overwhelm I would always uncomfortably encounter, whenever I'd walk into a very negative or noisy room. Finally, Doreen explains about those humans who experience head-on hunches and true gut feelings that foremost help others optimally to heal, when she writes: "We all have spiritual senses, so everyone has some degree of clairsentience."… And, then (gratefully-for-me also shares in regards to my need for really productive peacefulness), she says: "Becoming more clairsentient is a double-edged sword. It can mean that you feel everyone's emotions, whether you want to or not. It's also a little like having a hearing aid that picks up all sounds equally loudly. Still, most clairsentients with whom I talk see their sensitivity as more of a gift than a curse. And it *is* a gift, a gift from God!"

At this juncture, I could easily envision my surely, "Do it in ninety days duffel bag's very special contents" as being about halfway full. Where, intuitively too, I knew, that the only other subject I'd shied away from amongst willfully penning my *Life Is How YOU Look At It*, was stopping my cycle of stress eating whenever feeling truly lackluster and losing that last twenty pounds. Therefore, it would be two of Harley Pasternak's books: *The Body Reset Diet* and his revealing, *5 Factor Fitness,* that when accompanied by my new smoothie maker, were even in the most-ultimate of real time crunches, going to blitz me back into shape. Lastly, I found true comfort, that my final-packed prize inside would be my purple-covered Bible, as unlike a box of Cracker Jack where the best is at the bottom – it would only be by including our Lord's abundant blessings and asked-for verses mostly at the top, that would allow my sacred work of "S.P.A.R.K.L.E." to lead others toward His Light.

"Let your light so shine before men, that they may see your good works and glorify your Father in heaven."
Matthew 5:16
"NKJV™"

# WHEN "MRS. SAWYER" SUDDENLY NEEDED ME

(*** This story contains the first of my "Seven Special Sparklers.")

As you may recall from *Life IS How YOU Look At It,* Mrs. Sawyer was that awesome, lady-in-her-eighties who taught me how to cook. Moreover, while sweetly known for sporting both her much loved recipes and leather pocketbooks – she was also a shining example of "while some things change others stay the same."

    You see, it was August 2001, and Mrs. Sawyer's life would be forever altered by one extremely brazen lightning bolt, that would suddenly strike her Senior citizen's complex as she puttered around inside. Now, as the entire roof caught fire, she was forced to get out quickly, while only able to grab two things that truly mattered most. At the same time, her forever-on-a-mission family would not be far behind! As first off, it would be her paramedic oldest son then working as the Fire Coordinator, who would receive the 9-1-1 call to send backups to the scene. Here too, one of Mrs. Sawyer's treasured grandsons being the nearby town's Police Chief, would head on over to the area as well. On a lighter note, while being safely escorted away from all the smoke and soot activity - she clung ever-so-tightly to her rescued possessions, both being her famous recipe file and that favorite pocketbook. Next, as she watched in horror from a nearby store's adjoining lot, she could not help but shiver, over how her newly-hung wood cupboards had just wilted in the heat. Furthermore, her once so perfectly-pleated wardrobe was now seriously covered in soot. Yet foremost, she would be able only to face this sudden ordeal with courage - once seeing the comfort of her family's eyes. Then, as these helpless elders would find themselves struggling for some "Why did this have to happen, Lord?" answers, they would also find out later that day how a young and very heroic firefighter would sadly lose his fight for life.

Then, Mrs. Sawyer's path would dramatically change, once staying for several months as the guest of her grandson and his wife. When at the same time, she would continue to volunteer each Tuesday amidst knowing, "how just a bite her cinnamon-sprinkled coffee cake" would instantly soothe the pressures of our busy emergency room work. Meanwhile, we two would continue to savor our tapestried bond – that one of her magically picking right up where my late grandma had left off, amongst still sharing some stories together that made our hearts skip beats.

As time progressed, this retired nurse would next wrestle with some symptoms that she knew were just not right. Since, not only was she suffering from occasional flashbacks about that terrible fire – but now found herself plagued with some troubling heart palpitations as well. Yet, as all her medical tests optimally returned as healthy, she next enlightened me further how that "anxious feeling stored deep within her mindset" was from missing a place of her own! And truthfully, it was this very heart-wrenching issue, where I knew that THIS time I could help. See, it was as a single mom many years ago that after an awful flood in our mobile home area, I'd be unable to return home also for several days. Moreover, even as President Bill Clinton did declare this total nightmare to be a true State of Emergency, it would take me much longer than just a few days of that so-surreal inconvenience, to ever comfortably fall asleep again whenever heavy rains danced upon my roof.

Meanwhile, that next morning Mrs. Sawyer got into her car and drove over to check on the ongoing renovations, at the complex she called home. Likewise, as she'd snuck into the main entrance, no one seemed to notice that she was tiptoeing around. That was, until this sleuthing elder had made it to her own unit and found the door to be slightly ajar. When, just as she was admiring the framework of her newly-hung kitchen cupboards, a lady in a white hard hat suddenly emerged from the back. Here as well, she was more than happy to show Mrs. Sawyer all the work they had just done on her place. Incredibly also, how wonderful it felt just to be standing again, in the comfort-filled home that she so loved to live! But, as they headed toward the bathroom, this grateful lady now approaching her nineties, suddenly let out a gasp. Since, only days before that fateful fire broke out, Mrs. Sawyer had purchased a "still-in-the-package oak toilet seat" that was now nowhere in sight. Then, almost instantly, that lady in the white hard hat knew exactly where to go. After all, while sifting through the maintenance garage's storage area, she couldn't help but remember seeing a perfectly-wrapped oak toilet seat while wondering to whom it belonged. So, minutes later, these two "wildly on-a-mission ladies" would find themselves sprinting across the freshly-cut grass. They were headed to the nearby storage shed, to find that familiar part of her true patchwork that Mrs. Sawyer so terribly missed. Somehow too, once reunited with that had-to-have surfaced piece of cherished woodwork signaling such happier times – both her health issues fell to the wayside, while her faith was surely restored. And, just like my own late Grammie, she's encouraged me to always savor the simpler things within my struggles, and to remember to smile broadly whenever things get tough. Though in all honesty here, how many meticulous divas do you know, who would so humorously admit to driving around with a toilet seat in their trunk until they were destined to make it back home?

> "God sets up divine interventions just to bless us! When we are looking for our daily divine appointments, we find more than the excitement of being used by God. When we walk in the Spirit, we will find that God has preordained people to cross our path to be a blessing to us as well. There is no greater nourishment for our souls than to know that we are used by God in the midst of our daily life."
>
> ~ Sheri Rose Shepherd

# A SIMPLY SPECTACULAR STORY

"What lies behind us and what lies before us are small matters compared to what lies within us."
~ Ralph Waldo Emerson

One morning, shortly after beginning my E.R. workday, a woman arrived seeking me at my office. While it was not unusual for strangers to stop in that already knew my first name, she would further expand my horizons with her unusual request! Besides, during these past few years, when my many challenges seemed insurmountable, all I ever knew for sure was to cling foremost to my faith. Yet, upon willfully talking to "Lorna" I knew I wasn't alone with this concept. As what she had to say next, not only magnified my belief in miracles – but also made my hair stand up! You see, hanging behind my desk each day was a "very touching picture," the theme of whose sweet memories made both our faces smile! Awesomely too, this olive green and gold artwork was also entitled, *The Touch of The Master's Hand*. Somehow, once Lorna had laid eyes on this once-so-familiar passage, she just had to meet me firsthand. At this point, she would timely explain how "after all these years of searching for this warm-and-fuzzy print, appearing finally in horizontal" – she'd always kept the perfect spot available to hang it on her dining room wall. Better yet, she would share how even though this tapestry thread kept surfacing somehow, only in vertical variations – she knew if she prayed hard enough her treasured wish would come to light! Then, along these same lines she would make mention of a real miracle that awesomely occurred while she was attending a service at her church. You see, although her Dad's friend "Glenn," always struggled so shyly with his Tourette's syndrome amidst its awkward swearing and unusual antics, each time he recited *The Touch of The Master's Hand* all alone in front of the altar (a part of which appears at the end of this story) – it would go off without a glitch! Next, Lorna would try to offer me some money in exchange for owning this picture, and though truly a well-meant gesture, I would totally have to refuse! As next, she would need to be enlightened how it had been fatefully entrusted to me by a very special angel's family, and the only way I could part with it was to freely pass it along. After all, you may recall from my first book, *Life Is How YOU Look At It*, how my "priceless ragdoll, Ashleigh," had taught me to heal with true roses and tender reflections even though I'd really been hurt. Where over time also, this very large picture was all that I had to remember her by, once Mom and Sam's marriage sadly dissolved and they almost lived out on the streets. Moreover, as their many possessions were reduced to those now only within their backpacks, this mom Tricia, would next take it upon herself to last-time knock upon my door. Then, amidst fighting back tears as her bottom lip began to tremble, she'd share with me how I had just become the special owner of this preciously prized painting - which still has such an awesome way of reminding me, that no matter how rough our own storms get, God is ALWAYS at the helm! Finally, after making me promise to take good care of it, they headed out into the darkness. Then sadly here, though I'd offered them to stay with me until a hotel room could be paid for, Tricia's brave attempt to pursue the faith-filled power of Friendship, Family and Forgiveness - found her clasping hands with her two pre-teen daughters and leaving without looking back.

> "There is a light within each of us that can never be diminished or extinguished. It can only be obscured by forgetting who we are."
> ~ Deepak Chopra

*The Touch of The Master's Hand*

*Many a man with life out of tune,*
*And battered and scarred with sin,*
*Is auctioned cheap to the thoughtless crowd,*
*Much like the old violin.*
*But the Master comes,*
*and the foolish crowd*
*Never can quite understand*
*The worth of a soul and*
*The change that's wrought*
*By the touch of*
*The Master's hand.*

*~ Myra Brooks Welch*

# THE BEST BUCK I EVER SPENT

After becoming a first-time mom many moons ago, I paid a dollar for a charming piece of a poem that continues to hang in my hallway at home. Here, a tiny baby is portrayed sleeping peacefully, wrapped amidst her favorite blanket and being watched over by her teddy bear. While also edged in pastel rainbows with pink rose accents – this treasured "family heirloom" still radiates with love even to this day. Where gratefully, since forever focusing on the gift of keeping my parental priorities straight, this heartfelt advice has been worth its weight in gold!

"Rock-a-bye Baby"

Cleaning and scrubbing can wait 'til tomorrow
For babies grow up, we've learned to our sorrow…
So quiet down cobwebs, dust go to sleep,
I'm rocking my baby and babies don't keep.

~ By Ruth Hulbert Hamilton
~ adapted by Wendy Lyn

# THANK GOD FOR STRETCH MARKS

"You are Radiant Light, Eternal Love and Divine Grace in a Dance of Discovery."

~ Julie Parker

I can easily recall being an almost twenty-year-old and expecting with my first daughter, Michelle Marie. At this time, I weighed a little over one hundred pounds and gained less than twenty more throughout my entire pregnancy. While feeling great, I worked right up until a few days before she was born. Then, at my final prenatal exam my doctor confidently shared, how I should go into labor within the next twenty-four hours – and he was right on target. On this hot July night, I had an easy four-hour finale, as the timely pain shot worked well to take the edge off my contractions. Though truthfully here, the hardest part had been getting to the hospital A.S.A.P., as my year-older husband had to finish a new job's afternoon shift. Meanwhile, my designated chauffeur (and close friend, Jim), was begging me to make a pit-stop at Burger King's drive through for his long awaited dinner. Yet instead of getting some Whoppers-to-go, we high-tailed it onto the expressway to continue along with destiny's date. Needless to say, a "winless Jim" settled down in the tiled waiting room to watch the All Star baseball game – complete with a box of Lemonheads, and some Pepsi to wash them down with. Moreover, as the ice cream expert he was, along with the candy connoisseur he was studying to be, he was no stranger to witnessing any worthwhile scoop. And, today would be no exception, since he would also become my child's first, "artificial uncle," straight from the bench of his designated dugout.

Around eleven thirty p.m. our precious daughter was born. Amidst tears of joy, I counted ten tiny fingers and ticklish toes, while the hospital's camera crew snapped this quality family bonding moment. Little Michelle was perfect in my eyes, and the labor and delivery process was a piece of cake – or so I thought! Then, two days later, I left the hospital in my pre-pregnant jeans, while never giving a second thought to how easily they zipped up. Besides, I'd previously fit into anything right from the racks of every clothing store, including bikini bathing suits. So, why should post childbirth be any different?

To put it mildly, my second pregnancy was a real eye-opener as Bethany Nicole was as busy in my uterus as she continues to be today. And, she still has her days and nights mixed up excelling most in the darkest hours. (Meanwhile, her mom is exhausted by eight-thirty p.m. and even wears the "Grinch slippers" to prove it!) At the same time, I was ecstatic to learn that my friend "Kristi" was expecting right along with me – our estimated due dates being only six weeks apart. Wondrously too, there was no one else we'd rather share our non-stop nausea nightmares with. Where, as time progressed, our inside joke continued to be, what flavor of Rolaids would be the "color of the day." We even took bets on how many tablets it would take to squash our horrible heartburn – while also resting assured that some hair on our baby's heads would be one subject that we needn't lose any sleep over. Then, almost overnight, I became the proud owner of hips, thighs and stretch marks – and was quickly enlightened to the fact, that with each subsequent gestation everything expands then sags faster. On the flip side, this unique experience leaves us growing females to easily grasp how an elephant must feel as seemingly pregnant forever – while also becoming beyond grateful as well, for the invention of underwire!

Then, in January 1989, I went into premature labor, exactly one day earlier than my scheduled, six-weeks-before maternity leave. Luckily, my doctor was able to stop these contractions and allow me to return home. Besides, Uncle Jim was faithfully busy educating our older daughter Michelle, on the finer points of being five – from McDonald's French fries for breakfast, to Toys R Us field trips to purchase more messy stuff. At this point too, my five-foot-one frame tired easily, forcing me to become more of a couch potato as my ongoing leg pain really worsened and my due date was crawling closer. Meanwhile, Kristi delivered her first-born son in a forceps-first entrance, while also sparing me much of the exact play-by-play. Yet, how positive it is, that as a gesture of gestational courtesy we ultimately pregnant at the same time goddesses, smartly save out delivery room details until after we've all popped!

In my eighth month and during our final ultrasound, my obstetrician broke some frightening news to me. You see, although this baby girl was so much larger than my first, some of her very important organs seemed to be lagging behind. Then miraculously, even during this fearful sonogram our feisty daughter stole the show – as she somehow managed to flip over, suck her thumb and pee all at the same time for our Polaroid-like pleasure. Though on a more serious note, my ribs were being bruised from the inside out as Bethany kept on kicking me harder, just to get comfortable. At this juncture also, the doctor laid his cards on the table. While our much adored child faced being born disabled, he was more concerned about me carrying her fully to term. Then, he went on to explain, how my "body may actually burst" – causing instant death to me. How's that for a reality check? So foremost, as each twenty-four hours was critical for incubating our child, my feared-too-fragile structure was showing signs of sheer exhaustion. Now, my physician also guesstimated that our busy bundle was about eight-and-a half pounds at this time. He felt as well that I'd easily be able to deliver her without a C-section should the next few weeks run smooth. (Boy, how amazing it is that these "never-have-birthed before doctors" can tell us just how awesome our experience will be. Since awkwardly too, towards the end, we basically survive on bland chicken soup and saltine crackers amidst battling swollen "Flintstone feet" – until our front-and-center moment as a delivery room diva arrives!)

One week later, I was to be induced on a Friday. But regretfully nothing worked, as our baby was still not ready to "bless us with her busyness." Where instead, I returned home to my charming couch like a beached whale without any options – and just a seemingly forever case of Sciatica to show for my tiresome efforts. On the following Monday, I packed my overnight bag and headed off to be induced again. Besides, in my mind I knew, there would be no way I'd be returning home that evening, even if I had to perform my own C-section. After all, I was now past the point of being a patient, patient! As these powerful contractions progressed, I begged my doctor to break my water – only to find that as quick as it did I needed to get down to business! And, while thinking I would be a while, my doctor went out to scrub... Wrong! Here, as my baby descended the monitors dropped rapidly, making this whole experience worse as I knew how to read them. When suddenly, as Bethany's surely too-big shoulders got stuck within my smaller pelvis it was discovered as well, that her umbilical cord was wrapped around her neck. Meanwhile, as the nurses shoved my husband away from my side and all-out aided with my efforts, I was told only to breathe through several strong contractions. Then, once given the green light to push the room began to blur as I faded with fatigue, where the now very-noisy monitors began to plummet for both of us. In a heartbeat here, I also pleaded with God that if one of us was "meant to be heading home to heaven" to please let it be me! At this point something has to give – and that was our daughter's broken collarbone as she made her crying entrance. Though this time, amidst all the increased activity, I was unable to nurture my newborn, as the nurses quickly whisked her off to both stabilize her blood sugar and call in a bone specialist. Moreover, this whole whirlwind event had taken less than fifteen minutes.

    Shortly thereafter, as I lay trembling on the table – several thoughts flooded my mind at once. Where first, I reflected upon the fact that if I ever half-brained chose to have another baby, I could probably just sneeze and it would fall right out – basically bypassing the entire labor process. And, as my obstetrician continued to steadfastly suture, I totally suggested he "just sew everything shut." After all, I knew my natural childbirth days were over and

I was becoming a nun. Because I knew, if my ecstatic spouse was entertaining any ideas of fathering a son, it would be his turn next to suffer true frostbite in the stirrups.

Then, after resting comfortably in my room for a whopping eight minutes, the nurses made me rise and begin to walk the hallways. Where on this tiring occasion I wondered aloud to myself: "If any man who'd just passed a kidney stone through one of his tiniest orifices, is next forced right out of bed to run a marathon as well?" Yet, my discomfort was well worth it once arriving at the nursery window – where I now pressed my nose against the glass to get a better glimpse of our "little girl." Sweetly, as the only female amongst five boys, she appeared so precious under the lights, and was the longest in the room at almost twenty three inches in length. When to my further surprise, while heading back to my suite, I was stopped by two smiling nurses who questioned: "Gee Nancy, don't you hurt?" As obviously they knew by my petite frame, that delivering an almost ten-pound papoose had been no day at the beach. Though happily here, I was on a natural high while blissfully savoring how lucky Bethany and I both were - since only hours earlier our fate rested entirely in God's hands. Where truthfully too, the physical pain of my million stitches was not half as bad as the life-or-death outcome I'd been mentally forced to prepare for, prior to delivering our daughter. Besides, eating Motrin like tic tacs helped a lot too!

## THANK GOD FOR STRETCH MARKS PART II

About seven hours later, a bright-eyed Bethany Nicole found her way into Mommy's arms where I was in no hurry to let her go. Sadly, her tiny arm was pinned across her chest to help her collarbone heal quicker, a regimen I was told would continue for several weeks. Then, on first thought as we bonded, she was very heavy to carry and humorously resembled a Butterball turkey! Then, once our visitors left, I snuggled her close to my chest where she quickly fell asleep being comforted foremost, by the sound of my familiar heartbeat – just like my special Poppy had so lovingly done with me. While I caressed her full head of hair I couldn't help but notice the unique color combination of brown shades weaved amidst blonde shimmers on her totally spiked edges (while also unaware at the time that this exact hairstyle would be "my trademark" too in the years to come). Then, as my newest addition turned her head around to nuzzle in closer to my neck, I was in for an even bigger surprise! As here, I was shocked to discover a large purple bruise etched across her precious forehead, another painful reminder of our day's shared battle scars.

    Later that night, while relaxing alone my emotions flowed freely. As my mind next replayed the fast-moving frenzy of the day's events now in seriously slow motion, I honestly knew I was lucky to be alive. Moreover, I was overcome with such gratitude to God, since obviously He (amidst cheating death so far three times in my life), wasn't finished with me either. Meanwhile, I also promised myself to capture more "Mommy moments" – while mindfully cherishing my cherubs. Therefore, once feeling better I returned to work on a limited part-time schedule, though money was tight at times. Yet, it's amazing what you can learn to live on if your priorities are in the right place. Meanwhile, a happy Bethany settled right in at home, as her name means "house of poverty" anyway! Then, as previously envisioned our preschool days were excitedly filled with: nature walks, reading books and designing sculptures from Play-Doh, Candyland games, trips to the mall and Happy-meals-to-go! And, while these mother/daughter outings began when the girls were very small, we have yet to take them for granted today. Besides for all those had-enough days when I really needed a break, Uncle Jim and his sweet tooth would help out too – with everything from Dilly Bars right before dinner to petting farms, since he had now twice the spoiling to do!

    More recently also, while revisiting these precious scenarios amidst some long lost videos I had an amazing light-bulb moment.

You see, this mommy-hood memoir not only illuminated the importance of playtime at any age – it also had a profound effect on my postpartum perception of me. Where prior to this "near-miss," my greatest personal challenge seemed to be accepting my new shape unconditionally. Yet, over time too, I have discovered that I was far from alone in this negative thought pattern. As unfortunately, many women have confessed to feeling a sense of shame, even at the thought of their long time partners viewing their now surely-altered bodies, naked in the light of day. So instead, these once very daring ladies, choose to make love in the darkness – while buried under blankets just to get "it" over with. But, once my life flashed before my eyes on that day in the delivery room, I will forever see things differently. After all, God granted me an extra chance to unravel my uniqueness and give gratefully of my own gifts! Moreover, this wake-up call would also magnify the magnetism of being born a female, amidst cherishing forever the tapestry-threaded miracle of actually giving birth. Likewise, for those times in my past where my mate always felt that I should have looked a certain way always surfaced in the long run that I was in the wrong relationship to begin with. Incredibly too, I've also learned the hard way to see my own previously-thought figure flaws, in a new, refreshing light. Where positively also, although the days of being voted "Best Buns" in high school homeroom along with selecting bikinis right off the rack remain just flickers of my pre-baby past - I'm more content today to be wearing a one-piece leopard bathing suit.

Looking back now, my second pregnancy experience was a true blessing in disguise as it blissfully helped to pave the way towards this passionate, penning purpose, amongst now cradling myself with the self-love I would have once saved for somebody else. Yet, more important, by leaving the lights on everywhere, especially during lovemaking – we can all experience those magical "I Am Woman" moments much more often. Also, by getting creative, (from candles, to Calgon to campfires) you too, can develop an awesome appreciation for the beauty of being beside your beloved. Lastly, as my own once-fearful blankets now comfortably fall to the floor – my surely "chosen by Christ partner" will happily celebrate right along with me. You see, while sweetly knowing there is nowhere else that I would rather be – I wouldn't be snuggling beside him if I hadn't been saved by my stretch marks!

Bethany Nicole, ten days old.

*** The previous story also reminds me of a time when I too, as a playful child, would help make dessert over at Poppy's. As every time we would make my favorite strawberry flavor, I sweetly saw (amidst my really red-stained lips) that: "Life can be a lot like making Jell-O" - since we can choose to harden all alone in the darkness or poke and play along the way!

The Sweetness of Sisterhood.
(while at least in front of the camera!) –
Michelle age nine and Bethany almost four, 1993.

"The secret of change is to focus all of your energy, not in fighting the old, but building the new."
~ Socrates

*TRADING CONTROL FOR CAREFREE*
*(Please ask yourself the following questions) -*

*When was the last time you ...*

*Talked one-on-one with God or
thanked your guardian angels?
*Caught raindrops with your tongue?
*Sent someone's favorite flowers or
bought a present ... just because?
*Wallowed in a warm bubble bath
or went for a massage?
*Decided you were worth it,
even once you saw the price tag?
*Played "hooky" or actually used
one of your personal days?
*Laughed till tears ran down your face?
*Ate cotton candy, bobbed for apples
or slurped a Sno-cone treat?
*Slept naked or shared your pillow?
*Slow-danced on a street corner?
*Read a fortune cookie?
*Wore mismatched socks
and didn't care?
*Whistled instead of whined?
*Watched the splendor of the sunrise?
*Spent the day in your pajamas?
*Went sledding, skiing or made snow angels?

*Blew bubbles with your children?
*Asked exactly for what you needed
or said, "How can I help?"
*Gave away a prized possession?
*Kept a secret for so long, you
thought you'd actually burst?
*Rented a Jacuzzi suite?
*Stuck your finger in your birthday cake?
*Played Frisbee, Twister, Scrabble or Yahtzee?
*Took a moonlit walk and found the Big Dipper?
*Drank green Kool-Aid, Vernors or Nestle' Quik?
Stole that much-needed nap, or stayed up all night
listening, laughing, or loving?
*Wore your ragged jeans or ratty sneakers?
*Said "I Love You" and meant it?
*Baked homemade cinnamon rolls with frosting?
*Ran your fingers through your little one's hair
until they peacefully drifted to dreamland?
*Appreciated a rainbow or saw
"pictures" amongst the clouds?
*Complimented a coworker
or gave your boss a hug?
*Turned off your phone and pager,
to totally turn on your partner?
*Went to the Drive-in movies?
*Found an hour to finally do
what truly matters the most?
*Frolicked with your faithful pet?
*Prayed for someone who has been sick?
*Stopped apologizing to everyone,
for issues that aren't yours?
*Pitched a tent under the stars?
*Ate cereal for dinner?

*Noticed the chirping of birds, the vibrant color
of butterflies or the magnificence of mountains -
on your last business trip?
*Let the rain softly soothe you to sleep?
*Followed your heart - by placing that call,
penning a card, or packing
someone special in your suitcase?
*Gratefully paid your bills without grumbling,
as you timely wrote out their checks?
*Got lost in the library?
*Didn't make your bed?
*Kept your promises to those most precious,
no matter how petite?
*Made those necessary screening appointments
for medical and dental visits,
since self-preservation matters too?
*Sang along with the car radio
or church choir?
*Stopped by an antique shop
and picked up a piece of your past?
*Said "no" without explaining yourself?
*Hugged your children close
to your heartbeat or really
looked into your lover's eyes?
*Read that book you've always wanted to?
*Donated your time, or no-strings delivered,
the gift of whatever you're good at?

* And finally... Realized in the magic of a treasured moment -
there's nowhere else that you'd rather be?

        Now Ask Yourself: "Why not?"

"There are two kinds of people in the world: Givers and Takers. The takers may eat better, but the givers sleep better."

~ Marlo Thomas

# AS ONE DOOR OPENS, ANOTHER CLOSES -

A LESSON IN CHARITY, RIBBONS AND ROSES

A few years ago, I read about the importance of cleaning out my "personal clutter" in order to make more room for prosperity in my life. So, with nothing to lose, I embarked upon a journey to release those things that no longer served me – while also unaware of what a surprising outcome this shedding of stuff would all have. Then in a heartbeat, I sifted through those bigger boxes that were stored within my bedroom, as really clueless anyway to their unlabeled contents. Moreover, living life at "The Spa" (a.k.a. my mobile home) had not allowed for much storage space anyway. Next, I decided to save only those things that had truly special meaning or that I really intended to use. Here also, I found myself sorting through some old family photos, keeping only those representing happiness, while swiftly discarding those showing pain in anyone's eyes. It was at this point too, that I stumbled across my old high school picture, where when recalling my foremost wild-side antics, felt such a surge of reconnection with "her." After all, this dusty young lady held dear many dreams and desires, not so unlike those I had sweetly accomplished! Though, more any other feature I couldn't help but notice, how that favorite Avon gold heart necklace stayed so tightly clasped around my neck. While happily gifted to me by my now-gone Aunt Nan, it made me smile to think amidst our so total love of laughter, how much I've somehow matured. From, those rebellious times in my mid-teens, to discovering now as re-born woman how: "As long as my open heart rules over my opinionated head, a world of wisdom always appears when I choose to walk in grace and faith.

Next, my friend "Fifi" would show up (my special nickname for her after a seriously gone-wrong perm) with hot brownies and some ice cream to boot! Shortly thereafter, we would begin to lug out my old wedding gown box, from the darkness and the dust bunnies, under my youngest daughter's bed. And, while I tried it on and it still fit nearly twelve years later, we could not help but laugh at its winding silk train and whipped cream sleeves. Yet, while twirling around in front of the mirror, I was struck by a mind-blowing thought! While it is so easy for couples today to get married, it should be taught somewhere in our upbringing - that it's the cherished art of Friendship, Family and Forgiveness that helps them to stay that way.

Later that day, as I trudged this satin gown and its clumsy box out to the curb for tomorrow's trash pick-up it felt wonderful to surrender those inclement memories of "largely looking back," instead of willfully loving my life. When suddenly next, it began to rain a warm, summertime mix of such soothing raindrops as I stuck out my tongue to catch some, while misty steam also arose up from the ground.

Now, I was ready to tackle my clothes closets, while also feeling as though I had somehow saved these seemingly shadows of darkness, for surely last on my list. Since, like many other women these overstuffed contents consisted of my "Hafta-wears, wish-it-fit and oh, yuck it fits" collections! Meanwhile too (just like me), I regularly observed many majorly stressed out ladies appear sloppily dressed as they picked up their children from school – making us all look more like a "Jenny Jones search for moms needing makeovers," than that so perfect June Cleaver we'd all seen on TV. At this point too, I also learned how parting with the past isn't always easy. That was, until from those major fashion cobwebs of my closets emerged, that fitted stirrup pants and baggy sweater look – a flashback to my maternity days where I always felt clothed more frumpy than feminine. Moreover, since my youngest daughter, Beth was now over the age of ten, and my baby-itch urges had all about withered, I couldn't help but wonder "What EXACTLY am I holding onto these for?" Though, my intuitive answer came almost instantly, as the seemingly brave single mom I always portrayed in public, was seriously afraid of becoming a bag lady. To make matters worse, I foremost pictured myself at that age with only a few measly coins in my pocket and ragged clothes on my back – amidst no real game plan either, for gracefully growing old. Furthermore, as this stark realization contained some destitute scenes, I pledged to forever face this fear head-on, and courageously design my dreams!

Then, about twenty minutes later, many of my outfits had been divided into three piles: those for the Salvation Army, those for Thursday's garbage and those that needed some sewing. Where, when all was said and done, I was awestruck to discover that my soothing "comfort quilt connection theory's wisdom" carried over wondrously, to my wardrobe as well. As remarkably, among the clothes I'd resolved to keep were silky leopard-print robes, stunning purple dresses and lots of scarves accented with cherished roses galore! Incredibly too, with this purpose-filled task almost finished I thought my fateful mission was now in the clear. That was, until my eternally "favorite, yet far too big sweater" of glittered purple ribbons amidst bunches of pink and burgundy roses, next fell out of a box and unexpectedly landed right onto my foot. And, while for several minutes I really wanted to keep it, I then remembered the so-worldly thought of true prosperity behind my purging plight.

## RIBBONS AND ROSES – PART II

(*** This part contains the second of "Seven Special Sparklers" in the bag lady I met, Ruby.)

Throughout these times too, I would rapidly learn how everyone who crosses my path is never there by mistake. Even though sometimes, the gift amongst these encounters has me challenging my comfort zone! As on this particular day, once dropping off my unwanted things to the Salvation Army, I next headed over to another plaza, to pick up my list of things. (Yes, the very same parking lot where I'd met that "one heaven-sent angel while so-cluelessly penning my *Life Is How YOU Look At It* memoirs" – who'd pulled that huge amethyst rock from his pocket that helped to keep my concentration on course.) Now, it was years-later also, that "Ruby" entered the picture this day- complete with her totally ragged appearance and majorly toothless grin. And, while always flashing a mega-cavity filled smile, amidst a voice that totally stuttered and slurred each time that she spoke – made others around me who were so appalled by her looks keep commenting on how: "She truly made their skin crawl" with her unsightly presence. Yet, I on the other hand, was hugely intrigued by her bag lady insights – while choosing instead to lean in and listen instead of judging her harshly. Besides, what better way to confront our fears than to have them land right in our laps? Therefore, during our first conversation Ruby would "ask me my name, about where I worked and if I had any young children at home?" At the same time she would share with me, how her husband's name was "Rex" and that they were new to the Western New York area. Where in turn, I happily observed, how her eyes would always light up at the simpler things in life. After all, Ruby was never without a steaming hot cup of coffee - even if she had to mooch it for free from wherever these two would end up. Here too, while, she obviously needed someone to sympathize with all the heartbreak that littered her past, I couldn't help but wonder why she had somehow *singled out me*.

Then, on our second bump-in, between all the broken sentences and tears of sadness, I learned how both she and her wheelchair-bound husband truly treasured their one room hotel. Where, in all honesty, it had a soft place to sleep, a fridge for their food and heat to keep their feet warm. More important, their new home came equipped with its very own coffee maker, to sweetly enjoy their favorite treat. So here, just like sisters in a silhouette, I was spiritually reminded also how: life is really all about the little things if we stay grateful while we learn. As ironically, I too for years, had adjusted to a new way of living in my smaller mobile home behind our Poppy - (to the obvious disgust at times of those, like one of my cherished doctors who stayed so busy condemning my choices). Furthermore, while I can count my encounters with Ruby on less than one hand, what an impact her raspy and rosy outlook would have upon my once, "Oh, why me?" life!

The next time we met up, she was just leaving our local drug store and held some newly-purchased hair ties tightly in her hand. When, almost instantly she shared between loud sobs, how many years ago "the state had taken her daughter Linda away." Now, as a surge of tears now overcame both of us, she spoke such a heart-wrenching language I could more than understand. Since, it was actually that very morning that my oldest daughter had decided to go live with her Dad, even as the ink was still sadly drying on her "only hours-earlier court order" – where dangled promises of extra money and material goods truly appealed to her more. Here, as well, before Michelle would so happily pack, she would also illuminate me further as to why a life at "seemingly Disneyland local" was indeed the way to go. See, if truth be told, she was too embarrassed to admit where I lived, ride in my car or have her birthday parties over at my pool-less patio, because all her friends might not accept her if they REALLY knew how her mom lived. (Though, today we laugh, as it is I who has turned the tables since my stellar old-lady car, still runs better than that clunker she's kept through college!)

Then, surely when it came to Ruby she'd save my biggest awakening for last. As one Saturday morning I had planned to blitz right through the grocery store – but upon rounding the displays of fruits and flowers saw a real traffic jam up ahead. About the same time, I regretfully spotted both Ruby and Rex standing only about ten feet away. Where as no surprise also, she was busy stirring a hot sample of bulk food coffee with none other than her finger, removing it while dripping, and slurping it aloud. Here too, while so hoping not to be noticed (as after all I used to work here!) I simply prayed to God to seriously just let me slip on by. Though, like so obviously and eternally, the Lord wasn't finished with me either. Here, to my total mortification and by turning ever-so-slightly, Ruby would next grab on to my cart and announce happily to a growing crowd of onlookers, how "Miss Nancy" had come along too! Likewise, while the lines in this area weren't even moving, I had no choice but to hope for the best. Yet here also, I would be in for the shock of my life! As next, this "basically-ME-many-years-later-in-a-mirror, bag lady" would turn totally around to face me – wearing none other than my old, ribbons and roses sweater that I'd just sent to the Salvation Army! Where miraculously too, as that long line of customers began to clear the aisles, this light bulb moment so changed my life. And, although I can't begin to tell you what I bought that day, this fateful wake-up call would forever change the way that I do business. Since that very next week, I began to save loose change, started a 401k and now religiously shop with a list. Finally, while I never did see "sparkling" Ruby again, her mystical bag lady beauty, would blissfully so set me straight!

> "Do not forget to entertain strangers, for by so doing some have unwittingly entertained angels."
>
> ~ Hebrews 13:2
> "NKJV™"

# TAKING TIME OUT
# FOR GUARANTEED GIGGLES -

AND TIDBITS I'VE BEEN TOLD

*** Dr. Marc Klementowski is a tall, compassionate man with a heart as big as his smile. As luck would have it, he was on duty one morning when a days-mixed-up newborn came in for some care. While this so tiny preemie now slept peacefully in his car seat – we all marveled at the makings of this little mini-miracle. Especially since, he truly resembled a porcelain angel that we couldn't help but reach out and touch. Yet, even more amazing was the wondrous warmth that continued to encompass the room. As, once this special baby was headed towards home, our staff continued to exchange stories on the plusses and problems of parenthood - like "colicky-fussing, collarbone fractures and cooing fiercely at three a.m.!"

Then, Dr. Klementowski humorously confessed that even the "rigorous regimen of his residency was a piece of cake" compared to the demands of being a new daddy now twice over! Where, at this time too, he shared a truly touching account, from the blessing-filled branches of his wife's family tree. You see, in the early 1900's a premature infant was born to a couple with the signs of survival seriously stacked against him. Since fearing the worst, their doctor next suggested that this sad twosome return home, without the presence of their struggling son. Though, while refusing to give up hope, they brought their tiny bundle home and nestled him in a shoebox, right beside the never-ending warmth of their house's woodstove. Needless to say, his wife's grandfather then thrived, providing the cherished tapestry-thread that both his wife and now three growing daughters are ultimately based upon. Lastly, may this treasured tidbit leave each of us thankful for our own fortunate framework – that can only be explained as truly a gift from God and the angels above!

*** To know my friend Heather is to love her. After all, we met not only when she was transferred into my area, but when both our worlds were falling apart. Where, one day "us moms" just got to talking comfortably out on the porch, about all our pride-and-joy daughters and our ongoing dilemmas with men. Though, more than anything, while getting to know this inspiring sweetheart, (and also "sisterhood purple candle collector") exuded the steadfastness of her courage. Moreover, Heather's heart mirrors daily a belief system that has been ingrained deep within her sparkling spirit by two very devoted parents. And, although this wisdom would at times cause her to nearly misstep, she's sweetly managed to come out on top. Especially when amidst God's comforting promises of His grace and backing, both died within six months. Yet, previously also, her forever-husband would sadly leave my struggling friend at the height of her parents' illnesses, for someone with a well-known track record (from even within my own small circle) for snagging other's men. Though, while this female would also continue to flaunt in Heather's face that she'd seemingly stole her destined first love – we two continued to humbly take the high road amidst knowing, there's a very big difference in this world between those of class and crass.

Happily over the years, our friendship has continued to blossom, since built strongly on a cherished base of several cinder blocks laced with ribbons of love. Though, nothing would have prepared me for the laugh we would get when we both turned the age forty about ten years ago! As it was at that time, that another friend had just also become a grandma, while Heather herself was happily dating "the good-looking blonde guy" that I'd simply told her from a previous vision, was surely coming her way. Moreover, I was busy trying to birth my first book – a true collection of tender memoirs about real Misfits and realized miracles, while making my time for any love life, truly a thing of the past That was, until one morning when Heather approached me and suddenly shared how: "After all those nights of passion with her new beau, she may very well be pregnant and now so-humorously couldn't even begin to look at eggs!" Where next, while it would take a few minutes for both of us to even speak amidst our mirrored "Elmer Fudd Syndrome" – whereby, after already having two older daughters at home, the birth of her third one also has added only more joy to their lives.

Then, a few months after her youngest was born, Heather said that she now planned to high-tail it to an area hospital, and seriously get her tubes tied for sure! Yet, the biggest glitch was going to be who would be able to drive her, since her fiancé had a new boss that would only let him drop her off at home after the procedure was done. So, as you guessed it, even as Heather was worried that she would need to cancel – this scene also illuminated painfully in neon lights ten-fold for this only daughter, that both parents were now gone for good. Therefore, I knew, from our so-sisterly relationship how the saving grace of being her accomplice to this operation, was surely going to land on me.

Meanwhile, on the morning of Heather's surgery I arrived at the hospital to meet her, while never thinking twice about the last minute personal day I'd scored just to be there by her side. Yet, for me, I was no stranger to this facility either, as ever since my own upbringing I'd had some of my closest friends and family members employed also there for years. Therefore, as Heather was now in her procedure, I went out to make my rounds. But, not before I grabbed her warm and welcoming sweater, since the waiting area was so cold. Then, after trying a few different medicines for nausea once post-op, she was ready to both dress and go home. That was, until we searched high-and-low for her missing underwear, only to be humorously discovered much later, stuffed in the pocket of that sweater I'd stole! Finally, while this treasured memory still leaves us in stitches today, it also bears asking the laugh-out-loud question here: "When it comes to carrying around your personal business – who, could you trust the most with your stuff?"

*** While grocery shopping recently, I once again bumped into a "breath-of-fresh-air" gentleman, that I had crossed paths with many times before while going about my motherly errands. Where each time we connected, "Frank" radiated with happiness, whether alone or with his wife, "Evelyn" – leaving me always to feel really fortunate for the wonders of their wisdom! Then, on this afternoon, after answering Frank about both my job and my girls, I began to mention briefly about this newly-started section of my stories. At this point, his eyes lit up amid offering me a very valuable thirty-second tip to share with all my readers on surviving in any relationship amidst those times both tough and tender. Since, this treasured twosome have also taught classes for those Catholic couples ultimately planning to wed – Frank happily enlightened me here, with their own so-successful strategy for living harmoniously over the years. Next, he went on to share: "When you as a pair have a disagreement where there are still some unresolved issues and dismal feelings that won't dissipate" – simply lock your bedroom door and *get naked*. Then, once all your clothes are removed you should kneel down together and face each other, in the middle of your shared bed. Lastly, make the time here to look into the expressive eyes of your loved one and let the light of your love heal the hurt. While chuckling as well, Frank guarantees that surely one of two things will happen: you will either both burst into laughter during this lighthearted scenario, or find yourself cuddling in your sweetheart's arms after making passionate love. Yet, ultimately either avenue reaps the same results of being rapidly reacquainted with what truly matters the most – a "rippling richness of renewed romance" based on your mutual love and respect. Since graciously too, you can always choose laughter or love making over long, drawn out battles, with the added advantage (as my late Poppy would say) of "never going to bed angry."

***Lastly, I would like to thank my late aunt for sharing something with me that every time I encounter this type of situation, I can't help but coast on through! As one day, I was telling her that after about thirty-plus years of working with the public, and even many times, woefully facing the ongoing battle while dating over the years, of who's considered by some very judgmental others to be the in-crowd or the outlaws – she said something so amazing that I still value it today! You see, once I began to mention that two of my biggest beliefs since I began writing about light-bulb moments are that: "It doesn't take a degree to be decent," and "There is no hierarchy in Heaven for those who make life awful on Earth," she was listening very intently. Where next, while my "Aunt being my very special Aunt" she now humorously said something like: "Dealing daily with people like that, Nanny, is a lot like looking in a tea kettle, because most people are only seemingly nice to other's faces, then scrunch them up when they walk away." And, while this treasured thought has on so many days continued to soothe my wounded spirit (as I can actually hear at most times also, at a greater distance than others would even begin to know) - it keeps me laughing amidst their foremost immaturity, to warmly remember my own, once-childhood antics of making faces in the funhouse mirror or that old stainless steel tea kettle as well!

*** "Don't be distracted by criticism. Remember, the only taste of success some people have is when they take a bite out of you."

~ Zig Ziglar

# LIVING LIFE AS LOVABLE

Learn to let others love you, just because you're YOU. Not for what you can give them, do for them or twist yourself into being. Where surprisingly next, you'll sweetly uncover that loving someone isn't supposed to be a one-sided effort based on conditions of approval, or solely reserved for special occasions. Strive to let the walls down around your heart and watch a beautiful beam of blissfulness begin to beckon your being from all sources (since truly whatever you believe in your own little world, rebounds back ten-fold from the outside!) Then, notice the abundance of loving actions magnetically appearing from every direction, while delightfully discovering like a child busily burying their toes in warm sand at the beach that you can't help but dig in and enjoy it! Also, start accepting yourself for the illuminating individual that you are, while allowing those that you cherish to celebrate your true colors. Remember, that real love doesn't promote the unending presence of pain but mirrors instead the magnificence of miracles-in-the-making. Furthermore, upon examining "your previous passion patterns" if you find yourself repeatedly attracted to the same types of toxic scenarios – you can always take a spiritual time out and carve your way to a sweeter existence. Here too, try to retreat within your soul's sacred limits and explore your personal reasons for settling for less than you deserve amongst your everyday script of success. Instinctively as well, propel yourself onward to a healthier homecoming, based on the principle of never being too old to creatively change. Besides, the optimistically-oriented universe responds awesomely to those who graciously give thanks for everything from hard knocks to happiness! Meanwhile, continue to tell yourself regularly that "God doesn't make garbage" - as ultimately someone else's trash is genuinely another's treasure. When you overall realize that we all see things differently, and not everyone will approve of your outlook, that's truly o.k. As in the end, what will matter most is how you passionately portrayed your own self-worth, while focusing foremost more on fixing yourself versus finding fault with others. At this point, you may gracefully unleash your own God-gifted mission, becoming less of a ho-hum face in the crowd and more of a person you can face in the mirror. Willfully make a vow to revitalize – by getting a makeover, keeping exercise essential and feverishly fulfilling your bucket list with or without a mate. Likewise, it is only once we have "lit up our own loneliness" that true love can ever enhance us with - a never-settle-for-less-again, nurturing combination of: I'm me, (s)he's (s)he, we're we! Where positively now, this fresh outlook allows two whole beings to now beautifully blend while mindfully merging amongst their predestined paths. Here as well, you will rejoice in how your once, troubled-at-times history, becomes just a small speck in your sacred rebirth. As an added bonus, when you consciously promise to lighten your load of any lingering shame and guilt amongst taking real risks, the Lord's many gifts find that much-needed room to both miraculously multiply and permeate your personhood. Where, wondrously also "faith always finds a loophole" to send along that which we are missing the most – especially when we least expect it. Since, you as well, may have been that unwanted child, "uncaring" friend or unappreciated lover in the patchwork of your past. Yet, in all honesty, it is only by facing, forgiving and freeing these so negative-at-times thought patterns – that allows another's nurturing spirit well within our walls of desire to truly share our sunshine!

> ... "For every exciting success I've experienced, there have been many, many failures. But I can honestly say that I don't regret one risk I took on behalf of my real heart's desires, whether or not the outcome was what I had hoped. What regret I do feel is reserved for the times I backed away from a risk my true self was urging me to take."
>
> ~ Martha Beck

"If you love something set it free. If it comes back it's yours, if not it never was."

~ Richard Bach

# FATE DOESN'T FORGET

(This story contains the third of my "Seven Special Sparklers," in my ever-sweet friend, Rosa.)

"Rosa" met "David" while away at college in Norfolk, Virginia in 1990. He was an All-American wrestler who enjoyed both dating and "hanging out with his buds," amid the crazy campus party scene. Yet, little did Rosa know, in just one single star-struck night, her fateful destiny would be forever changed. You see, as she entered the college bar one evening, her gaze suddenly connected across the room with a man she had never noticed before. Then, once their eyes interlocked, she was "flooded with an internal warmth" that radiated right to her soul! Where, even today she still believes that she majorly fell in love with him during that first mesmerizing glance. Then, from that night on they passionately dated for about a year, though David painfully continued to pursue other women. While also true to his character, this young-at-heart ladies' man was always accompanied by his tell-tale red Jeep – as Rosa still recalls how her heart would pound happily each time she spotted him cruising around the campus.

One evening, after graduation, David stopped by Rosa's place only to say goodbye – as she would be staying another year to finish up her studies. Meanwhile, David had no idea how deeply she cared for him. Besides, since he was actively choosing to leave her behind for various new ventures – they never even bothered to exchange addresses or phone numbers. Decidedly at this moment, Rosa didn't want to push, instead allowing him to walk out of her life without divulging her secret. Where actually, she was still very much in love with him, yet was willing to let him go as these feelings were not mutual.

Seven years later, Rosa was finishing up Chiropractic Grad School in Atlanta, Georgia, where she was also working as a waitress at a happening local sports bar. Where, like every other afternoon, she was absorbed in cleaning off her tables – although on this day the usually busy restaurant was atypically empty of hungry appetites. Suddenly, her gaze shifted to a "flash of activity," that caught her eye from another side of the building. Surprisingly too, through this group of windows that were separated every few feet by several wooden panels of restaurant walls, Rosa quickly got a glimpse of a red Jeep entering the parking lot, that just seemed to sparkle in the sunlight. Then, unexpectedly here, her thoughts traveled back to those carefree college days of so romantically dating David in Virginia. Now, as her heartfelt memories continued to materialize, she squinted to focus further upon this fine, young man, who was now slowly heading towards this establishment's entrance. "Hmmm... He looks like David," she thought to herself. Now excitedly, as he entered the sports bar her hunch was confirmed – as this truly was her long-lost love! Next, amidst disbelief he asked, "Rosa, is that you?" Where, in response to this realization, they both hugged and kissed as their hearts pounded profusely once again in synchronicity. Rosa also learned that David had been living in Atlanta also for the past three years and was busy running his own business, a sports and entertainment company for athletes. Even more remarkable was the fact that they both shared the same circle of friends, yet had never crossed paths again until this latest date with destiny. Here, after tenderly catching up, they did exchange phone numbers, where throughout the next year David left many unanswered messages on Rosa's machine. He truly ached to convince her how much she'd been missed, and that he really wanted to spend time with her exclusively as a couple. Yet, those "ugly flashbacks from being hurt before by her ex-heartthrob" continued to flood her unforgiving mind. So ultimately, she chose to reduce the risk of getting hurt again and instead ignored all of his calls.

About one year after their surprise meeting, Rosa had a change of heart. She then called David out of the blue – where they decided to meet one evening at his upscale apartment. In looking back now, she joyfully recalls the elevator ride up to his penthouse as that not-too-familiar pounding of her heart faithfully accompanied her as well. When remarkably here, she realized, that she could no longer deny her pent-up feelings, as she only felt like this while in David's comforting presence. Intuitively too, Rosa knew that her own heart had been spiritually steering her towards him after all these years. Likewise too, she was now willing to listen, while celebrating also how complete their companionship magically made her feel. Next, after riding up to the top spot, she nervously knocked on his door. Once open here, the sweet David-she-remembered eagerly embraced her, allowing her free-flowing passion to finally prevail. Moreover, as Rosa stepped inside, she could not help but notice how empty his surroundings were. Then, without hesitation David explained that he would be leaving in a few months again to further advance his career options. And, after recently placing his belongings in storage, he soon would be staying with some friends – until his planned departure off to the New York City area to fatefully watch his future unfold. Yet, foremost at this point neither really cared about the furnishings, making them the farthest thing on their minds. Instead, they opted to spend this time "willfully reconnecting" with sweet romance on the rugs. Where ultimately too, their bodies long-last united, confirming something that their senses had known years before – they were Soul Mates from the start!

From that electrifying "elevator night" on, they now dated exclusively and were inseparable for the next two months. Then, after vacating his penthouse and staying with his pals, David was ready to move now to New York. As previously planned also, in another date with destiny, Rosa would stay behind again to finish up her school. Where, as an added surprise she would discover that she was shockingly carrying his child – to which David's overall response was truly less than thrilled. Moreover, although this baby was unplanned, Rosa decided to keep her. And, while continuing along with all her exams, she faithfully toted her new little bundle to her last two months of classes – awesomely wrapping up her doctorate degree without David once again, so painfully not in the picture.

After graduation, Rosa and the baby returned to her hometown, aiming to live with her parents for about a year. It was here, that I experienced a "comfort-quilt connection with her" at my own chiropractor's office. As throughout my visits, how her eyes would more than sparkle each time that she would mention, her cherished commutes to New York City – for some quality family bonding time with her treasured beau and tiny baby! Yet, cautiously too, Rosa would now explain how she was planning to make both a very conscious and correct choice as far as furthering her relationship with David would go. After all, she now had two hearts to look out for and to not let them both get hurt. Here too, she was hopeful that if they were able to rekindle their romance it would be on the freedom of desired togetherness - and not from the deemed forced responsibilities to their new little dependent. Steadfastly as well, Rosa was secure enough to allow David the space to figure out what he wanted, amidst staying focused on her own priorities too. Therefore, while patiently preferring not to rush their nurturing efforts, she religiously vowed more than anything, to never-again come last in his life. Even as her mind so regularly missed his presence and her heart begged her to stay. When, at this point, Rosa radiated explicitly with joy after returning from each romantic hiatus that were occurring more frequently now. Meanwhile, David yearned to bring the love of his life back into his heart and his home as a full time family. Somehow, with the added bonus of nurturing "Daddy's little girl" – he'd learned that he was a lucky man now twice over. Then during the

Christmas season of 1999, David asked Rosa to relocate to the New York City area for good. It was here that I lost track of her, only to be updated by my cherished chiropractor that she was living happily now as part of a family, after forever squashing her fear of failure with a fresh start and some real forgiveness.

## FATE DOESN'T FORGET – PART II

> "If you want a happy ending that depends, of course, on where you stop your story."
> ~ Orson Welles

Many years later, as I began to ponder these passages, I wanted Rosa's sparkling spirit to be part of my precious pages. Especially since, she'd dared to set free her soul mate not once but twice – trusting more in the magic of perfect timing over their perfect match. Besides, by taking a time out to invest in both her self-worth and soul's worth, amid totally surrendering her heart throb of a man, Rosa proudly evolved into a self-assured woman. Moreover, she was completely convinced, that David would only return amongst the framework of her path - if God Himself truly guided his future back home to her fluttering heart.

Months later, after incurring several roadblocks while I tried to track down Rosa's local family, I was randomly given the phone number of a thought-to-be uncle from someone who'd suddenly crossed my path. Where successfully too, after calling him, amidst some feelings of real "warm-fuzzies," this this man next shared positively with me that my timing couldn't be more perfect. As next, he enlightened me also, with the welcome news of Rosa's and David's spring wedding, planned for that upcoming weekend, and religiously promised to forward along my name and address as well. Here too, while continuing on with this second book's so larger-than-me mission, I rested assured that the true turnout of reestablishing our reconnection lay totally within the Lord's hands. Though somehow, while eternally practicing patience, several weeks had passed and I still hadn't managed to interact with Rosa to get her much-desired update. Yes, the same one I had been so "spiritually informed" while meditating was going to grace these pages. Then, early one Friday, I made an unexpected appointment at my chiropractor's office, while finding myself needing an additional adjustment. At this time, since rarely having any mornings free I also found myself wondering just how busy his office might be. Where upon arriving I was placed in a room rather quickly and began to soothingly meditate. Moreover, while resting, comfortably here, my concentration suddenly shifted to a cheerful conversation that echoed in the hallway – that ultimately Rosa's mom was having in the room across from me! Likewise, since having met her once before, I hopped up to hopefully cement our connection further – where her pleasant mother was happy to not only share her daughter's phone number, but some positive news as well. Lastly, she excitedly explained, that her daughter would be coming back shortly to the Western New York area for a visit, and that this very special couple's wedding had been beyond beautiful as well.

A few weeks later, I touched base with Rosa at her mother's house, amid excitedly telling her how lucky I've felt to connect with her in my constantly-changing life. As not only did she possess the gift of such a healing touch in her hands to seriously soothe my stress load – but has also successfully shown me as well, that we can all experience "real love" – if we are willing to both rest faithfully in the arms of angels and also wait for God's right time. Then gratefully, Rosa continued to fill in the gaps since we had seen each other last. Where delightfully too, in the spring of March 2000, David whisked her off for a romantic trip in the Bahamas – and while surrounded by breathtaking scenery, he proposed one night on the beach. Awesomely as well, as their eyes again flickered with such feelings of familiarity, Rosa accepted his ring wholeheartedly, amidst being truly amazed that her family had managed to pull this huge secret off without her ever knowing!

## FATE DOESN'T FORGET – PART III

In January 2001, another baby girl was born adding to their bliss, and providing a new little playmate for their other, older princess. Where today, fate finds Rosa happily married and working part time, amidst the raising of her two girls. Likewise, with the love of her life now beside her full time, her life overflows with fulfillment. Moreover, she always giggles childishly, as she mentions how, "she and David still look into each other's eyes and melt," just like they did with that first college glance. Also, although much busier at this time with both our hair-raising happenings amongst the rearing of her budding toddlers and my blooming teenagers, Rosa and I have successfully managed to still stay in touch. Where wondrously too, while continuing to share our illuminating endeavors from over those last eighteen months, we remain ever-so- grateful for those special goose bumps we get whenever we wallow along the same wavelength. Then next, I humbly informed her by phone, how while driving one morning during the summer of 2001 – it was "suddenly suggested spiritually to me, to stop by my friend, Jared's house" for a hot cup of tea. Where, once seated at his kitchen table, I was giftedly guided to ask him for his newspaper (something I rarely read while nurturing my creativity to consciously avoid any heightened negativity). Now, humorously here, my fair-weathered friend suddenly informed me too, how he had just used about half of its printed pages to empty some soggy, coffee grounds into – and was now unsure of how much could actually be retrieved from his garbage. So, forever knowing as I do, that someone else's trash is always another's enlightening treasure, I now separated out the salvageable part, to figure out exactly what it was that I'd been (not-so-discreetly) urged to uncover! When here, amidst the non-messy main section, I optimally discovered the radiating warmth of Rosa and David's weeks-earlier wedding picture – while intuitively knowing also that their story, was the one to work on next.

Yet, for this newly-combined couple, nothing could top the not-soon-to-be-forgotten challenge in resilience that truly appeared right before their eyes in the fall of that same year. Furthermore, although the honeymoon was still far from over – their tried and true love would unexpectedly this time, be put to the ultimate test. Where, mindfully resulting as well in a fearfully learned Life Lesson mixing both their wedding vows with what's forever most important – they too, would learn to treasure that even during the toughest of times God truly has our backs. You see, it was September 10, 2001 and David would find himself working inside the walls of The World Trade Center in New York City – at exactly one day earlier to the very hour, of this once-thought sturdy structure's, so unnecessary demise. Then, weeks later, when we solemnly connected amid the aftermath of "America's worst-ever wake-up call I can ever remember" that true terrorism sadly exists - Rosa's voice still quivered with "What-if he'd actually been in there one day later?" thoughts as I tried to calm her fears. Likewise, the reality of this whole situation left this meant-to-be pair echoing loudly, that they would never again take for granted the miracle of their love. Moreover, after realizing how primarily pursuing a hafta-have lifestyle, comes with some really huge price tags, echoes also the sparkling fact that: "We United States citizens are truly a bonded family who will forever honor those brave heroes' memories from that Tuesday, September 11, who made the ultimate sacrifice for our Country's safety and never again made it home."

In the aftermath of all this, both Rosa and David have since solidly promised to keep both their needs and nuptials sacred – as they were truly shown firsthand, to foremost live and love more in the privilege of the present. Then, amid seeing how "there are no guarantees in life that their glimmers of hoped-for tomorrows, will gloriously turn into today" – they also really hug, hear, and help each other without conditions, while reaping the obvious treasures of whatever they've regally sown. Here too, both Rosa and I know that we were brought together to truly mirror how, our worlds had each become more peaceful when we both learned to appreciate with an abundance of passion, another's amazing presence. Gratefully as well, from Rosa's now-open heart it has genuinely sunk in that: "Sometimes soul mates may need to say goodbye to mindfully grow, grieve and graduate" – though may find themselves back together, once the Lord's timing is right. After all, successfully striving for everything special on Earth means nothing, without someone special to share it with. Where rewardingly, amongst our last conversation, Rosa grasped perfectly my previously-awakened concept of: "celebrating actively our comfort quilt connections"– with an enlightening example of her own! You see, at this point, she excitedly explained how more recently she and David had moved into a new house. And, although money seemed tight, she had some very high hopes of beautifully decorating her daughters' shared bedroom. Wondrously too, upon mentioning this wish "while on the phone with her mother" – Rosa was awestruck by her reply. As unknown to her for all these years, her mom had safely kept from her childhood, that very cherished set of twin pink rosebud bedspreads to now warmly wrap her own dreamers in. Though, even more amazing to my sweet friend was her heartfelt reaction, when receiving this preciously-sent package, days later in the mail. Where here, as we talked, she continued to gush with gratefulness over suddenly realizing that all she'd once only wished about as a starry-eyed girl (while securely snuggled under those so-soft covers), was delightfully now, happily-ever-after how she was lovingly living today! Where sentimentally next, she also remarked that she hoped that those "special pink rosebuds would bestow the same love and luck on the lives of her own little angels." Yet, most cherished to me is how Rosa has confirmed that my divinely-guided thoughts remain right on target even before my pages go to print. Since, awesomely also today, after previously working with God to sacredly reach out and touch my readers, I have sweetly tasted success! Simply put too,

*Nancy Loss*

Rosa has benefited beautifully from my belief that our childhood tapestry threads are meant to be handed down, not hidden away – after becoming unafraid herself to let others know her needs. Finally, Rosa and I still always end our comfy conversations with her forever letting me know, how she and David are still thriving. Above all here, while never taking for granted again the gifts of our miracles, our mates and our mothers – we should all be so blessed to have such happiness to come home to!

> "Soulmates are those one in a million people who have the perfect chemistry. They know what makes their partner cry and they know what makes their partner smile. They bring joy to each other's life because they see the best in each other. They are each other's voice and strength. They have immense faith in their relationship and they stand firmly together in the toughest of times."
>
> ~ Aarti Khurana

"You can't ask for what you want unless you know what it is. A lot of people don't know what they want or they want much less than they deserve. First, you have to figure out what you want. Second, you have to decide that you deserve it. Third, you have to believe you can get it. And fourth, you have to have the guts to ask for it."

~ Barbara D'Angelis

# ANSWERS ALWAYS FROM MY FAVORITE AUTHOR

(***This story contains the fourth of my "Seven Special Sparklers" – Barbara D'Angelis.)

    I am living proof that when the student is ready, the teacher appears. As wondrously, since becoming more spiritually sensitive over the years – I have been "instantly illuminated with answers" anytime that I am drawn to a Barbara D'Angelis book. This scenario started about sixteen years ago when her *"Real Moments"* first crossed my path. Where at this time, as I randomly leafed through the shelves of my favorite bookstore, I can recall feeling both overwhelmed and underappreciated. Then, while in search of what was lacking in my life, this tempting title caught my eye, amidst a sudden sensation of mindfulness. Where, incredibly here, not only did *Real Moments* leave me grateful for Barbara's guidance, it became one of the precious pieces that forever-changed my perspective. Sweetly, once experiencing this encounter, I have since realized that the biggest thing missing from my life was ME, and unwrapping all the mini miracles God kept hoping that I'd see! Yet, while also knowing over the years that I had endured more "raw hurt" than real happiness, I began to overall question "Why?" That's when God answered me back one day with – "No, Why NOT you, Missy, Life Is How YOU Look At It." Besides, as I reflected back throughout those years, appearing far more tough than tender – the illuminating fact remained, that the times I had the least I learned the most and loved the best! Since Barbara writes only with heartfelt honesty, she had helped to heal my heartstrings as well. While no longer able to ignore my own repetitive issues, I began to face my own ripples of reflection in the messages of her memoirs. Where at times I've cried right along with her as the wilderness-searching "sisters," we two had somehow become. Like her as well, I was no stranger to self-sabotage, amidst thinking I should exist a certain way just because someone else had said so. Yet, after sustaining two failed marriages, feeling abandoned by my own father's elective absence and struggling to withstand the deaths of cherished friends and family members who sadly moved along much sooner than they should have – I have finally seen the light! As now, staying somewhere that I'm not appreciated serves to only to stand in my way. On another positive note, Barbara taught me to carefully listen to the soft-spoken whispers of my own inner child – who needed to be heard and now regularly comes out to play. As she wrote candidly about her own airplane encounter with "little Bethany" (delightfully my own daughter's name), she prepared me wonderfully for when my own mini-mirror, Arielle, appeared on my front porch, allowing me to bask in the beauty of colorful butterflies just by noticing nature. As my soul work continued I learned to cherish the contents of her books finding her insights more illuminating as I mindfully surrendered my shortcomings. You see, I too, was a flood survivor, gave more than I got in relationships, and was always looking for love "somewhere out there." But, once mastering my sweet motto, I saw that, "if I face the world from a point of self- love first, things can't help but flow together not constantly fall apart!" I also found that by letting go of those who only function amid their own drama, we create the necessary room to attract more of the nurturing others who have our best interests at heart. Over time also, I've learned to welcome the warmth of that that "intuitive sensation" as God speaks directly to me – making all those once-thought random experiences, now truly extra rewarding! Though, most of all, I could relate to Barbara's rush of inner restlessness and fear of discovering what this feeling really was. Likewise, I couldn't help but notice how my treasured teachers appeared from all walks of life, becoming my guides to gratefulness even as I once wandered around oblivious to the obvious. Where, over time too, I took to heart the value of some true spiritual messages, serene meditations and very soothing massages from these timeless-to-me tutors. Remarkably too, as more wished-for beings "willfully keep appearing just like faithful flashlights to illuminate the way amongst the wonders of our life lessons," I've discovered that we are divinely way more talented than the day-to-day failures others try to relentlessly keep pointing out.

Then here also, something incredible occurred! The magic that Barbara's books had unveiled through the years finally "clicked" and added to the cherished miracles in my now faith-based existence, amongst opening my eyes, ears and heart to the power of a passion-filled lifestyle. When, sweetly here, and after praying to God, I decided to take a much-needed time out to explore my beliefs about love. When suddenly, I saw, it "wasn't so much that I was unlovable" but that I was not loving my life enough or letting myself be loved! So, at this juncture, I consciously replaced sadness with sunshine, caution with courage and painful people with peaceful surroundings amidst my new-found authenticity and a slew of non-stop options. After all, nothing in life appears passion-filled until we pledge to get passionate about personal fulfillment. Where next, with Barbara's insightful assistance I became "emotionally naked" and learned a whole new way to communicate with touch, talk and tears. Over time also, when I chose to mindfully surrender and really merge in the moment with anyone or anything that purposely crossed my path, unconditional love began to ooze from everywhere. I even changed my outlook towards my hectic Emergency Room work days from beyond stressful to going home grateful. Though still today, I have a tough time understanding why most of us suppress our bottled-up feelings or beckoning fantasies, until we are told that we only have six months to live. As truthfully, I see daily that life doesn't give out rain checks. And, since there is no guarantee of taking care of things tomorrow, TODAY is the time to take that treasured trip or tell others how much they are loved! Moreover, as those we adore have an unexpected way of being here one minute and in heaven the next – it's much better to make peace, make love and make memories in the magic of here and now. Though, all of this began as Barbara's purple book, *Passion,* accompanied me home from the bookstore next, where never before had I read such wonderfully written words! Now, as I practiced being passionate amidst a backdrop of mentor mirrors, it became almost effortless, once I focused on appreciating my experiences more than I ever truly imagined. To my further credit, the more lovingly I lived, the more I was blessed with new family, new friends and new faith in my future.

Then along came *Are You The One For Me?* – which aided in sparking a much-needed overhaul of my sad-but-true practice, of settling for less in my love life. Likewise, while taking this book's questions and quizzes seriously, I evolved a winner in my own eyes, by learning (in my words as well) to "date with dignity," replacing those happiness-stealers with higher standards. Meanwhile, Barbara's way with wisdom taught me most how the right love will: heal more than hurt, give more than get and survive more than stagnate. At this moment too, I began to deal with some previously-suppressed childhood memories that had started to divulge ever-so-slowly from my subconscious. Yet, even as these torrid thoughts continued to trickle, I was once again shown by her gone-first example that these awakenings would not amount to anything while wrapped in God's comforting guidance that I couldn't courageously handle head-on!

Shortly thereafter, my Poppy passed away while being comfortably cradled in the arms of hospice care. Where, amidst struggling with my sorrow over losing the man who'd loved me the most, I was once again drawn to bring out *Real Moments*. On this heartfelt refresher course, Barbara reminded me as well, of our universal need as humans to "dance with our grief" – something the ever-ballerina in me really needed to hear. Next, when I purposely chose to take a serious breather from nurturing others and tune into my own neglected needs, I saw by giving my all to everyone else I had forgotten to save some for me. Then, I reminisced through our times together, listened to music that I loved and made a collage of Poppy's pictures to brighten my entrance, as I thankfully come home each night. Likewise, while still finding a way to eternally savor his smile, I awesomely stumbled upon Barbara's sparkling advice of: "Whatever the issue, LOVE is the answer." Remarkably too, when I expressed these pent-up tears, happier thoughts evolved and my heart felt ten times lighter – while premonitions, prayers and positives resurfaced amidst reflections, reality and rainbows!

## ANSWERS ALWAYS FROM MY FAVORITE AUTHOR PART II -

From pesky fish to favored passions!

As I continued to meditate often, I kept visualizing a single goldfish sadly stuck inside a fishbowl. When suddenly, this illuminating image seemed to be following me everywhere! From the pages of our daily newspaper, to a "never-flipped-before calendar" hanging in one of our busiest work offices, and then on a larger-than-life cardboard sign covering an entire storefront window! Where somehow, I couldn't help but notice how this not so subtle fish was certainly here for the long haul. Meanwhile, my mind shifted back to attending an unexpected Deepak Chopra talk about fifteen years ago at our local Artpark Theater. Where for only a ten dollar ticket, as he addressed the audience from center stage I just loved what I heard! At this point, he suggested something to the effect that: "We should each 'expand our horizons' when seeking answers from the universe." While next, he provided wonderful examples of how billboard signs, magazine articles, television shows and radio announcements were some ways he had discovered his own divine destiny amidst major media magic! (Moreover, he'd already taught me well from his wisdom-filled books, to always carry an unwrinkled fifty dollar bill in my wallet to always attract abundance, and to be sure to take care of my body by applying oils daily and to mindfully address timely whatever else might hurt). Then, minutes later, as I left my seat to "make my own intermission" – I excitedly discovered Deepak standing alone on the all brick patio, amidst nature's soothing rain and nighttime's real serenity. Where, even more remarkable, when I grasped his hand and our eyes interlocked, I felt a true surge of warmth as I thanked him for redirecting my reasoning. Since, in the form of a gently spoken sentence, he had gratefully shifted my focus, as I now face each challenge without expecting limitations but with limitless opportunities for both growth and goodwill.

Once home that eventful evening, I had the urge to call up my friend, "Lisa," where I next aimlessly asked her aloud: "What possible awakening could this persistent goldfish have in store for my heightened spirit?" As this conversation continued, we humorously discussed several more angles of this made-for-me-vision, where I could foremost relate to feeling as trapped in my surroundings as this forlorn fish seemed to be. Since in the "fishbowl of my own existence" I could actively envision the life I wished to enjoy from outside the glass exterior. Here too, Lisa and I giggled together when I matter-of-factly mentioned how this wayward, fish-out-of-water was obviously mirroring me! I now confessed that I didn't know if I was supposed to break out of the bowl or bravely jump out of the top (as both moves were considered risky), to begin my sacred quest towards living out a life that I loved. Besides, I knew, the hardest obstacle would be leaving behind the warmth of the water that I had forever grown accustomed to, by having to "let go of my life preservers." After all, Poppy or my faithful pals had always gone fishing with me. While also sensing how I had outgrown this cramped existence and was craving to explore a whole new opportunity, I could not help but ponder to Lisa: "What was it I was destined to do?" Where, lightheartedly as we talked, she reminded me of my "Answers Always for the Asking" connection to any of Barbara's books. Then, this trusty friend from fifth grade surprisingly shared, how my much-loved author's newest work had recently been released – as she'd just refreshingly viewed her expertise on a talk show two days earlier! So, the next morning while feeling half-crazy, I headed off to my favorite bookstore to see what Barbara D'Angelis could have possibly written about goldfish. Yet, when I entered the best-sellers area, Barbara's *Secrets About Life Every Woman Should Know* was right on the new-release rack to greet me. Likewise, after becoming its proud owner I eagerly took this book home and began to leaf through the pages, in search of my latest spiritual wisdom regarding what was waterlogging my life. Soon, as the "speed reader I am", my sought out answer appeared on page fifty. Here, Barbara then makes reference to a wonderful anecdote about the courage to change. She next tells of how a little boy empties his four pet goldfish from their tiny fishbowl into the waiting waters or the family's larger bathtub, until "Jimmy" had successfully cleaned up their quarters. After happily finishing, he knelt down by the bathtub and then called out to his mother in amazement! To his surprise, although these finally free fish had the whole tub to explore, they eternally remained fixated in one close-knit circle. Where, like us Earthly beings, these adaptable animals remained sedentary in their surroundings – choosing the calmness of comfort over the chaos of change. At the same time, I knew, that there was something bigger and better that I too was avoiding by intentionally running scared.

    Meanwhile, as my pen began to blissfully gush into a blank composition book (that was proudly inherited from my late Poppy's unwanted-by-the-others belongings), I knew my intuition was beckoning me to begin dabbling in the manuscripts I'd once only dreamed about! Here too, I vividly recalled a spiritual palm reading from about eighteen months earlier, where Serena talked openly of how I had "gifted thumbs" – and would be creating something beautiful down the road. For years as well (and as I've previously mentioned in my sweetly published *Life Is How YOU Look At It*), my psychic step mom Lucy, would always smile and say: "You really should write that book, Nance. You've learned a lot along the way." Yet, there were a million reasons I could come up with not to. Needing to assist Poppy, raising my girls "properly" and working too many hours amidst maintaining a spotless house, just to name a few. Though, I was Superwoman by day, I was even more spiritually drained by night – by allowing my thoughts of penning these precious memoirs to take a back seat to everything else. Then, since my faithful prompting and that pesky fish weren't about to stop pestering my personhood, I passionately prepared to sink or swim! Besides, my girls were getting older now, Poppy lay peacefully at home in heaven and my workload had become more balanced – amidst the maid that I'd boringly become. As my journal work continued, I discovered how I was purposely avoiding the unknown I faced, to become a truly successful author/mermaid, on a desired three-book mission. So, it was at this exact moment, that I dared to dive in anyway, and began to design an outline of at least fifty-plus people who have deeply enriched my existence, amidst knowing that our merged, lived-to-tell journeys would unleash miracles in others' lives. And, with each story "I nurture till newborn," I feel as excited as the first time I felt my own unborn daughters uniquely move around inside of me. This awakening process has allowed me to gasp fully Barbara's forever, "giving birth to something wonderful" philosophy- besides the gifts of my own girls and without post-baby stretch marks! Where, like her also I have learned who my friends are as I approach the halfway point. These are the supportive ones who keep the texts and emails coming (even if I read them at 2 a.m.), or teasingly remind me to ultimately "come up for air" as we haven't talked in months! On the other hand, the Energy Vampires in my life can now only vent their ongoing issues to my voicemail, since my Poppy had thankfully taught me as well, how anything worth having is worth doing all the hard work. Though in reality, while I've chosen to replace their consistent crises with my need to be creative, I can only hope that someday after they each forgive me – they'll divinely reach for their own rainbows and strive to S.P.A.R.K.L.E.as well. Above all as my chosen family continue to read my works, cheer me on and add nurturing fuel to my faith-filled charisma, I feel so fortunate to have found my niche! Where suddenly too, as I forged along full of questions about "proof-reading, publishing and paying for this" on only a single mom's salary, my thoughts next wavered to mindfully wishing that Barbara D'Angelis could provide me with her lived and learned know-how, this one last lucky time. Then, to my surprise, a pamphlet arrived at my house from the mailing list that I'd so-surreally signed up for at Deepak Chopra's only months earlier talk. Where upon opening it I found that my favorite author's cherished book collection and website information were both delightfully detailed inside! Next, as I called the enclosed number in the hopes of acquiring her speaking schedule, I was sadly informed that my favorite author had no engagements booked any time soon. Yet, the nice lady I was speaking with provided access to another place that Barbara had been known to give previous lectures, though she was not planning to be there either, in the near future as well. However, I was enlightened that between the flight fees, hotel room, car rental and cost of her conference it could run me close to one thousand dollars! Therefore, like everything else in my life, I turned this thought over to the Lord's "let-it-be timing" – while knowing inside as well, if this trip was meant to be taken it would find a way to come to light.

Nancy Loss

# ANSWERS ALWAYS FROM MY FAVORITE AUTHOR – PART III

From True Awareness to Actualization

About two weeks later in September 2001, my intuitive rumbling returned with a vengeance, amidst waking me out of a deep sleep. As I sat up in bed and looked one-eyed at the clock, I became instantly aware that my previously-set alarm would be going off in about two minutes. Then as I leaned back against my pillows to silently ponder what it was "the spirit world was so desperately trying to tell me," my clock radio came on loudly amongst an advertisement about a local women's fair. Where above all they announced, how "the featured inspirational speaker would be author Barbara D'Angelis from California" – for an affordable fee of just five bucks and ultimately sponsored by my previous employer!

Needless to say, the week before the workshop, I feverishly pulled some all-nighters to prepare pieces of my manuscript. Here as well, I experienced my first case of writer's block only hours before our so spectacular (I hoped!) happening. Yet, once fired up and focused amid putting my pen to the thirsty paper, once again did me proud! While time ticked on, I finally finished for her my own heartfelt history, in true anticipation of our upcoming encounter. Then, once seated in the arena, amongst scores of others who valued Barbara's motivational magic, I patiently prayed for the chance to openly thank her – as I now forever dare to openly dawdle, in always-mine-for-the-asking mindfulness. Where next, she appeared in the audience, while also dressed in purple (the enlightening color that usually spells success in my life) and began to mix and mingle. Furthermore, while I headed up the aisle to approach her that "steady flutter of butterflies" in my stomach, was suddenly replaced with blissfully being on the brink of something big! Now, as I happily introduced myself and handed her a folder of passion-filled pages, I discovered her to be the type of down to Earth teacher, who was as easy to talk to as she was to treasure.

Then, I tearfully thanked her from the bottom of my heart for "being the best ten dollars I'd spent on my spirit" – including five of them several years ago on the written comforts of *Real Moments*, to five more at this moment to let her know how she'd helped to change my life. Next, as I handed over my favorite book, *Secrets About Love Every Woman Should K*now in the hopes of having it autographed, I also forwarded her a letter, I'd penned enclosed with lots of love. Meanwhile, Barbara hugged me tightly while telling me too, that she had sensed that: "There would be someone special that she would be meeting at this workshop" while needing to confront also head-on just to even be here, her sudden fear of flying on any airplane - since those both recent and senseless September 11th (2001) attacks. And wondrously, if truth be told, as that "warmly-envisioned inspiration" appeared to be none other than me – I was totally thrilled to realize how we had truly come full circle. As remarkably, after all these years of mirroring to me the rewards of her tender teachings, I was so touched to have blissfully manifested both my own "Back-at-you, Barbara, realization" and Real Moments reflection!

Shortly thereafter, as Barbara took to the stage, I was quickly enlightened that my Life Lessons in Loving are truly never-ending, as she appeared to be as beautiful in person as in the magical print of her books. Sweetly too, after hearing her speak on that October afternoon, I have since taken to heart five more of her tried-and-true strategies. Especially for all of those lackluster times filled with way more struggles than smiles! Where above all, as Barbara spoke eloquently about the so sometimes heart wrenching subjects of: happily living, healthily loving and hopelessly letting go – I absorbed once again from her gifted guidance as I jotted them down, that which I honestly needed to hear:

1) "A good woman knows not to waste her love."
2) "Some people cannot take in the richness of your love."
3) "Love will blossom like the rosebush – when planted in the right place."

4) "If you love someone more than they love themselves, they'll eventually hate you for it – that's not your failure, as it's not your job."

More recently too, while seeking out some solid advice on ultimately surrendering those once thought to be "the sun, the moon and the stars" of my own expanding universe, it was by timely reviewing the now-weathered pages of Barbara's *Secrets About Love Every Woman Should Know* that awakened my assertiveness again! By successfully freeing as well, those who were mindfully (or miserably) weighing down my wings – I courageously comprehended that: Sometimes we must willfully let go of others, to be able to grow more ourselves. I also found that once I was willing to stop "running away from all that I wasn't," and rejoice instead in all I will be, I can always rely on my own awesome answers which lie eternally wrapped within me.

Yet lastly, as Barbara spoke freely of her first-ever manuscript returning home from the editor amidst scores of red slashes and restructured sentences; I've been able to relate most to her fifth and final point. Where as always, she captivated our audience with another lived-and-learned sentiment of: "You have to 'suck' at something first, to finally become good at it." And, while humorously shedding a whole new light on my own sucked-at-times situations (from non-productive actions, to not-deserving-of-me partners, to totally needing help manuscripts), I'm now totally convinced that I cannot expect others to be honest with me until they become willing to explore their own truths. Moreover in the end, while embarking along this once-untraveled path to becoming a genuine "Sparkle Specialist," there's one thing I know for sure. When this Princess of Passion blissfully bonded with the Heiress of Honesty that enlightening afternoon, I saw that God's Gifted Hands had greatly assisted in this Higher-self success story. Where, in the spirit of answered prayers, I ecstatically witnessed this heartfelt exchange become my most treasured Real Moment ever!

"You are the snowflake in human form, designed with precision, created to add beauty and grace wherever you are. You have been instilled with a spark of divinity, which if nurtured can accomplish great and wondrous things."

~ Deepak Chopra

"There are two ways of spreading light: to be the candle or the mirror that reflects it."
~Edith Wharton

# FROM FEARFUL TO FRUITFUL – WHILE LEARNING TO LAUGH AGAIN

Incredibly, the pages of the previous memoir would not be the first time I could count on Lisa's love of logic to light my way out of a crunch. You see, many years ago I would find myself struggling amidst a "limited lifestyle" – as most behaviors seemingly routine to others, had somehow become really stressful to me. And, as my world closed in further with more "what-ifs and worries," I began to curtail many cherished activities, from dancing to driving, and shopping to socializing without having a clue as to what was really the culprit! Where somehow too, even getting a haircut, riding in an elevator or attending a typical church service was sadly too much for me. While heaven forbid, I'd have a doctor or dentist appointment as my knees would more-than-tremble making it easier to just stay home. Then, over time too, I began to trade hyperventilation for having fun, by always trying to prevent something horrible from happening. Yet, if worse came to worse and I had to "white knuckle" it through one of these worse-case scenarios, I would eternally hope in the moment, that no one else would be able to detect the ever-so-gripping fears I was secretly held prisoner to. Besides, I even worked (if you want to call it that!) in a very busy grocery store, where really strong customer service skills were such a must to secure our paychecks. Though luckily, on one such chaotic workday, my seemingly shrinking situation would never be the same.

Remarkably, it would be at this time of real upheaval, that Lisa would originally reenter my world. After all, I hadn't touched base with her tenderness since trading our high school diplomas for all that we thought adulthood had to offer. Happily here also, I found myself at peace by how easily our conversation flowed, as though we'd never lost touch to begin with! Moreover, Lisa seemed more amazed at my (apparent) ability to maintain such a busload of busyness – from steady management work amid being a mom, to taking time out for my marriage and me. Where next, I thought aloud, how "I was truly surprised to not have run into her sooner." Likewise, in stopping to listen about her restricted existence – I would instantly learn some very explicit reasons why so very special Lisa, had seemingly fallen off the face of the Earth. Since softly, she now whispered to my perked-up ears how she'd been "battling recurrent Panic Attacks" – making her primarily unable to work, drive long distances or be seen largely in public without the likes of "somebody safe." Then, at this very moment, I felt a surge of warmth strike my heart – while knowing Lisa's enlightening honesty had just gifted me, with some real tools for taking back me! Now within minutes, my own truths were exposed – as I next explained to her, that things are not always what they seem. We then exchanged a kindred laugh over the obvious dilemma that neither of our at-home mates knew how much we'd been struggling amidst the once-simple. Finally, to both our delights we would agree to become each other's "cheerleaders" – and were quick to discover that with bold confrontation of these once-nagging issues came nothing but positive change.

Willfully, the next several weeks would be solidly spent researching the subject of Panic Attacks - where the more I learned about stress reduction the more I wanted to know. Here too, Lisa would become my brave "driving instructor" as I then next managed to take her tiny, blue Dodge Omni up over the area speed bumps and sweetly even over a few blocks as well. More important, within months of my merge-with-fear outings, I was back to being on the road by myself! When also, during one laid-back weekend (where I was actually *learning* to take personal days) something truly magical happened. While flipping through the TV channels, I would ultimately find myself blessed with more anxiety-melting facts. Where, to my surprise, a beautiful lady appeared who had not only managed to beat her own Agoraphobia, but had survived to tell her tale! Miraculously too, this much wished-for angel was Lucinda Bassett, whose before-my-eyes excerpts from "The Midwest Center" would also help to show me the way (even in small baby steps) toward striving for wholeness again. And, within a week of nervously dialing their "800 number" I was enrolled in their home-study course. Then, one by one a cassette tape would arrive to help me to courageously adjust to these changes. I was even given the name of a truly been-there-before-me, supportive staff member to submit all my homework to. Meanwhile here, "Jamielynn" would become very dear to me – while making my willful efforts to diminish my boundaries, well worth all the months of hard work. Besides, the more restrictions I faced with fearlessness the faster they seemed to retreat!

Several months later, I confessed to Jamielynn about my fear of making a total fool of myself as the frazzled Maid of Honor at my only sister's wedding. But naturally now, this bird on a balcony also managed to assure me that I could even make it through this never-been-to-church in-years issue, by tackling more of my negative worries with tried and true techniques. To my delight too, she simply taught me to seriously "envision the worst," then to mix large doses of laughter amidst all the hyped up dread. When, to my further credit amid practicing my Positive Dialogue tape, I not only aced little sister, Becky's wedding hitch-free, but was ready to take on the world. Wondrously too, with both Lisa and Jamielynn giving me such an infinite supply of "You-go-girl" support, my once limited agenda went from woefully being very boring, to whatever I wanted it to be. In time too, by really raising the bar on my risk-taking behavior, I was having the time of my life! Since almost overnight, I went from avoiding all doctors to working right alongside them, by taking a created job promotion in the Emergency area I loved. Furthermore, as my existing fears were erased my own faith was enriched, whereby knowing I'd been enlightened, kept me grateful beyond belief (while also excitedly learning last-minute, how even Santa still exists!). Here as well, once my major stress load was replaced by mindfully savoring life – the art of soothing meditation mixed with prayer became like second nature to me. Then, as more positives really prevailed- riding in an elevator wasn't so awful, public speaking a piece of cake and those once-dreaded appointments from haircuts to getting my teeth cleaned became pleasurable, not postponed. Awesomely too, amidst all of these life-altering growth spurts the team of both Lisa and Jamielynn continued to stay in touch, with their very special mix of laughter, letters and love. Likewise, the more I evolved into my own safe haven – the more I was thankful for their open hearts.

Yet, down the road it would also be Jamielynn, who would one day point out (just like my "old" and wisdom-filled English teacher, Miss Pontecorvo!) my somehow gifted way with words. She also requested to be able to use some of my vulnerably-penned letters in part of her new Driving encouragement tape. Here as well, she invited me way back then, to be yet another "Attacking Anxiety success story" – by appearing live in New York City, to share my own awakening journey on Lifetime Network's, talk show *Attitudes*. Though, sadly next, my aversion to being discovered would only be second-bested by the boycott of any airplane and also avoiding one area bridge. As at this point, I truly believed, that I could never be an inspiration to others until I was CURED of all the above. Therefore, even as Jamielynn tirelessly suggested that I could even travel by train to get my story across, I continued to stick to my guns. Yet, in looking back now, I can't help but wonder how things might have been different, if I'd only taken this woman's words at their worth, instead of just dragging my feet. In retrospect too, it's even more important to leave those once-heavy hurdles behind us and have some fun in the here and now. In closing, though there have been times when I've really missed sweet Jamielynn's supportive sparkle through the years, I have also found out firsthand - that becoming fearless is not something that we fully conquer, but will confront for the rest of our lives. And, it really doesn't hurt to have some laughs along the way!

To My Cherished Readers:

- *What opportunities have you bypassed as well, by being too afraid to act?
- *Could you also "reach out to others" based on Life Lessons that you have learned?
- *If you decided to share your story, what kind of stage would need to be set? One of true highlights of divine intervention or the dreariness of total hum-drum?
- *Do you think I've since flown in an airplane or driven over that scary bridge?

"The biggest mistake you can make in life is continually fearing that you'll make one."
~ Elbert Hubbard

# THE DAY I DROVE THAT SCARY BRIDGE

If there's one thing I've learned throughout this book writing mission, is that our fears don't perish until we choose to pursue them. Besides, it was hard to feel overall successful with this still "so-wimpy bridge issue" still hanging over my head. Therefore, I planned a well-thought out strategy to tackle this huge-to-me hurdle for the very next spring day! After all, my fiancé and I had already set our sights on some great-priced carpet, located in a really big warehouse and about half an hour away. Where, as no surprise too, the easiest route to getting there would be up and over that "scary bridge." So positively, on that very morning as the sun now shone brightly before me – I sat prayerfully behind the steering wheel ready to leave my past behind. I was also happy to have my "supportive honey" in the passenger's seat beside me – since the Respiratory Therapist he also is, would (now so-humorously) be there to assist me, if my self-caused hyperventilating episodes even thought they would win this war. Moreover, it was "Allen" who had once so-awesomely also helped me, to alleviate by simply listening after losing my treasured Grammie, long ago to Emphysema - my fear of large oxygen tanks. Besides, I thought, what better companion to travel with, than having one who can save your life? Then, once getting some highway travel tips from Allen, I brought my sunglasses up to my face - before heading off in the direction to seriously confront that steel bridge that had for years held my thoughts captive. Where within minutes here, I sailed easily up and over it, while feeling the whole time like a winner – with nothing but a "surely now I can take on anything" outlook up ahead! Yet, the main thing here I learned was that: "In as fast as I was going, I had no time to waste on fear" - making this confronting with courage venture such a wonderful way to let go.

> "I trust life to be wonderful. I see only good ahead of me."
>
> ~ Louise L. Hay

"To love and be loved is to feel the sun from both sides."

~ David Viscott

# WHEN "THE ANGEL" ENDED UP BEING ME

(*** This story contains my "fifth Special Sparkler" in a tribute to young, Michael Torres.)

It was July 6, 2004, and I was heading downstairs after checking on the kids and changing into my pajamas. Upon reaching the living room, I gratefully smiled at the sight of my boyfriend all engrossed in his computer – while also knowing the night-and-day schedules we kept, were at times what helped us "click" best. After all, we'd come a long way in almost two years. From once being, two divorced people ever afraid to date again, to now being two single-parents-in-separate-school-districts determined to make our love work. Next, as I breezed by the clock, I noticed the time to be about eleven p.m. Though, as I passed by the television, I was struck by an overwhelming urge to turn on the nightly news. "How weird?," I thought, as I had made a promise to myself not to purposely wallow in any more negativity – after working all day as an Emergency Room Secretary (on roller blades) who just couldn't wait to relax! Besides, I'd been struggling for years to get my dream books off the ground – all aimed at enlightening others as they seek to heal their own hearts. And, since this crazy lifestyle left so little room for extras, I knew better than to ignore "God's callings" any way in which they came! So, as fate would have it, I clicked on the remote – only to find one of my favorite Emergency Room Physicians struggling amidst his own tears. At the same time, I would abruptly learn how his twenty-one-year-old son, Michael, had just been killed as a U.S. Marine over in Iraq. Here, as Dr. Torres' obvious pain hit right home to my heartstrings, it also unleashed "a minefield" of mixed emotions for me! You see, today was no ordinary day for me either. It was also my daughter's twenty-first birthday, who had at times spent her hardly-home years, purposely out of the area and painfully out of touch. Yet, as our really strong-willed kids would both welcome early adulthood, "Doc" and I would attempt to still show them the way. Moreover, while we would both agree through the years that productive parenthood wasn't always popular – we luckily learned too, that taking the time out to really listen, was as important as loving them through thick and thin. Somehow too, since we dedicated (though at times "dissed" parents) each stood witness to watching people die every day, our faithful staff's children belonged to all of us. Therefore, "our Michael" would be no exception, as I would always send his phone calls back to the doctor's desk, once taking a minute to catch up myself. Then, Doc would swiftly curtail his agenda just to hear his soldier son's voice. While the news from Iraq was not always positive, I could tell that this Air Force Physician was really proud of his son's patriotism. Likewise, he'd also helped to long-distance raise this so-determined young man, surely not afraid to turn his dreams into destiny. But, it was also this shining reality that made Michael's untimely death across the miles so hard to swallow amidst dad's grief. Sadly too, Doc and I had already experienced so much of "the stuff that dreams aren't made of" – from surviving childhood negatives to all-out crumbling marriages with continued setbacks in court. So, at this point I knew I just had to do something.

First off, I called Dr. Torres' voicemail and left a brief, but encouraging message surrounded in peace and prayers. Next, I asked the Lord to supply him the strength to accompany Michael's war-torn body back, to the family's hometown in Texas – where a full military service would be held, within the very next week. Then, with this "mission of mercy" supposedly complete, I headed back upstairs. To this time, meditate by candlelight on those things that make me most grateful. Yet, obviously God wasn't finished with me either, as I now found myself tossing and turning while tucked within my covers. Next, in my drifting mind I reflected back to those times when I too, had lost someone so dear that I thought my heart would surely shatter. This especially rang true for the time I had lost my grandfather, a magical combination of both a wonderful father figure and the wind beneath my wings. And, after returning to my hospital job after my Poppy's out-of-state burial, I would miraculously see as well, how the spiritual "outreach of Earthly angels," aren't always saved for everyone else! You see, at this inclement moment and while driving to work that morning, I practiced how I was going to "stay very professional" amidst my sudden loss of family – versus letting others see how scared I was from losing the man I trusted in most. After all, I had truly been taught since my childhood to smile at any cost, and to outwardly express any conflicting emotions only behind closed doors. Though, this day would become a true turning point for me, since I would honestly be made whole again by a surely "in-the-right-place-at-the-right-time-man", who would intuitively know my needs. That was the summer of 2001, and that man was Dr. Mike Torres!

As the story goes, I began my usual work duties by bringing lots more of our physician's paperwork over to their already overstuffed mailboxes. At the same time Doc would be leaving the lounge with his usual cup of half-slurped coffee. Then, without saying a word as I rounded the corner he extended his arms out to me. To my surprise, as this "star-spangled secretary" attempted to keep my composure, I ended up seriously soaking his lab coat with lots of pent-up tears. Now, while Doc held me tightly to his chest until there was no more grief to gush – he then assured me firmly how there would be better times ahead. Now, with my head cupped in his hands, he further explained how God would take care of my fear of eternally being abandoned in part, by leaning on the blessed family we had somehow all become. Then, as he returned to work with that huge (yet unexplained) "wet spot" residing all over his shoulder, I couldn't help but all-out giggle at his unconditional antics. As what a far cry for me, from always being the one to pass the Kleenex! Besides, I knew, that Doc's whispered wisdom was exactly what I needed to both "let down my guard and then let others in" – even if it did take me years of tiny baby steps and brave Michael's misfortune to begin to see the light. Furthermore, as I now lay snuggled beside my sleeping boyfriend, I felt I never would have been able to love him with such authenticity, if I hadn't taken the time to genuinely grieve out first. Lastly, amidst eyes that were feeling heavy, I went over the list that I hoped to accomplish on my finally-here vacation then faded off to sleep.

## WHEN "THE ANGEL ENDED UP BEING ME" – PART II

Upon arising the next morning, my supposed plans would unfold much differently – where it would also be made crystal clear to me, it is not I, who controls my true course. As surprisingly, once dressed and all done with breakfast – I would be "told" to grab my favorite journal, fuzzy blanket and some fruit cups - and spend the day down at Niagara Falls. Then, ten minutes later, amidst an "all things happen for a reason" mindset – I found myself naturally navigating behind the wheel of my car and not asking any more questions. At this moment also, I recalled witnessing an "Oprah" show as she shared heartwarmingly with her viewers about a remarkable happening that occurred while all alone in her home. You see, here, she was suddenly overcome by a spiritual sensation to travel to Africa – to truly help improve the education of some seriously less fortunate kids. Where incredibly too, I saw how the awesome journey of manifesting miracles is alive and well in all of us. Especially, when we make the all-out choice to follow our destiny just like young Michael Torres did! When somehow next, it dawned on me that: "While we have those dreams that we hope to accomplish" – did anyone ever just lay it on the line that tomorrow may be too late? Finally, many hours later amongst a fading skyline of pastel stripes, a straight-from-my-soul work of poetry evolved paying tribute to the fallen soldier I will surely never forget. And, when I drove home that day, a soothing combination of both exhaustion and exhilaration – I would be spiritually enlightened as well here, that my compassionate work for Michael was still far from complete.

The following day would be Wednesday, where I would next be driving to a party store plaza – only after rising early enough to add some touches to this rough draft. Then, once arriving at this store's entrance, I immediately zoned in on the "recently reduced" Fourth of July section. Then here, a 9 x 12 inch flag caught my eye made of shimmering red and white garland, amid a stunning blue background with stars. Where, from the instant I saw it, I was more-than-reminded of the "sparkling Michael" I so mindfully missed. Next, I also selected for his grieving father, a flag-covered photo album and a special CD collection of patriotic lyrics – honoring all those legendary soldiers who'd given their lives along the way. Though, in passing by the silver picture frames (one of which I had really hoped to purchase), I found their everyday asking price to be more than my proposed budget. Finally, I picked up some metallic gift wrap and made my way to the cashier. As hopefully, I had a few more days to work with to get this heroic tribute into Doc's truly healing hands. Meanwhile, once back at work I stopped at Kmart one night, to eyeball more photo frames. And, while the previous year may have been really ugly for the ailing empire of Martha Stewart, I left their feeling like a millionaire – once securing her largest, silver edition for the awesome price of under four bucks. Sweetly too, while still unknown to me in these sacred travels, the best blessing was yet to come!

# WHEN "THE ANGEL ENDED UP BEING ME – PART III

Somehow, with only twenty four hours left to get this gift all the way to Doc's now out-of-town workplace, I was still minus one very necessary touch that I could easily envision but could not seem to find. Then, amidst my hectic E.R. workday, I called my sister, Becky, who was more-than-happy to chime in with the name of a nearby store. So, with fingers crossed I wished the owner might just be willing to part with "one of her tell-tale silver plate holders" that would make my memoir complete. Yet, once arriving at this shop, the teen clerk behind the counter would learn all about the reason for my mission, though would also sadly have to inform me how her boss had gone for the day. Then, together we'd both begin our search throughout for that small, silver display piece – that would forever hold young Michael's "proven fearlessness, freshly typed upon special cloud-covered paper" firmly against the garland flag. When minutes later, after checking all the counters, candles and crevices – we found this silver have-to- have, in the front window after all! Where next, as the clerk would share how this piece was "not for sale" – I begged her to please either call her manager swiftly at home or simply turn her head so I could "steal it." (Besides, who says that wallowing amidst divine intervention doesn't come with some what-if risks?) Therefore, as she dialed the phone to get her boss on the line, I silently prayed for the best. Moreover, I knew, I only had a total of eight dollars with me – three that had been in my purse all along, and five from an unexpected "tip" only hours earlier, as my special doctor "Meister" had unexpectedly needed some lunch. To my relief, as God would sweetly have it, the store's owner had a heart made of gold and sold me that rare-find silver plate holder, for only five dollars plus tax. Moreover, the last leg of this spiritual scavenger hunt would find me counting once again on my sister, Becky (the always eternal saver of the seemingly unimportant), living only three minutes away! Likewise, once parked and perched upon her porch, she would give me her pondering "So, what are you doing here?"

look. Though laughably too, after all these years of being my little sister, one would think she'd stop questioning my intuitive life's work. While next, I let Becky in on a little secret. Her house contained the exact box I needed to transport Michael's miraculous legacy to the mourning family he loved. Then, without further hesitation, she headed off into the basement – only to return shortly with an empty DVD box filled with Styrofoam peanuts as well. Where finally, Becky gift wrapped my "awakened awareness" of what Michael had gratefully done for our country in a blanket of red, white and blue.

The next afternoon, I would be accompanied by my trusty boyfriend, as we placed Michael's forget-me-not message into the trembling hands of his father, my friend. And, though few words were exchanged here between us, its reality made such perfect sense. You see, while any person may be called upon to do such explicit "Angel work" – it is a true rarity indeed to see this outreach come full circle. As wondrously, both Doc and I had become the healing wonders who'd helped alleviate each other's grief! Then, as I hugged him goodbye amidst assuring him that we would be attending Saturday's local memorial mass, I was struck by an unusual thought. Since my own father had once so painfully managed to opt right out of my life – Doc would be the perfect man to gratefully walk me down the aisle, should I ever choose to get married again. (Though from previously had conversations, we both humorously knew, that for either of us to ever take "that walk again" Niagara Falls would probably freeze over first!)

Upon arriving at the church for Michael's scheduled memorial service, there was a soothing array of familiar faces and many uniformed soldiers as well. Here too, their Minister would encourage young Michael's parents "to focus less on the empty seat at their tables" and more on the family memories they shared. But suddenly, amidst this "parenthood all put in perspective," there was not a dry eye in the place. At the same time, as my heartfelt tears would begin to gush, my boyfriend would reach over warmly to tenderly grasp my hand. Where next, this magical move made me think about how "people truly take each other for granted"- until we are one day faced with the real harshness that our loved ones will never come home! Meanwhile, after this insightful service wrapped up, we all headed off to the church's basement for some special refreshments and support for Doc. Though here as always, he was full of surprises – as we found him to be getting married sometime again next spring. Then shortly thereafter, we would embark on the forty-five minute ride home, where "Allen" would suggest that I take a short nap before going on with our day. Yet, while I was still somewhat mortified that he'd seen me cry almost a river of tears, I knew this must be the magic of what love is made of, as he'd sweetly managed to pick up and protect me right where my strength had left off.

Once getting that much-needed rest, I would next jump in the shower as Allen returned from the store. Where here, he would suggest that we show up late to a family gathering and get lost at Niagara Falls first. So, like two "high-schoolers playing hooky" we headed off to the land that I love. Within minutes, my overworked senses were instantly soothed as the sun warmed my face with its timeless glory – while reminding me also how thankful I was for my seemingly heaven-sent partner to simplify all the stress. When suddenly, amidst refreshing breezes and brazen waters, I was in for a shocking surprise! Just as we were about to approach our favorite place for a picnic Allen got down on one knee and proposed! Yet truthfully, while we both knew that he had already purchased the sparking ring that we adored, the "perfect time" still had never come up. That was until THIS very day when, "We willfully became a couple, who had learned to emotionally white water raft!" Moreover, even today when I'm missing young Michael, I think of some things that make me smile. Finally, while his father then laughably "took the plunge" again, on none other than the real April Fool's Day - I optimally discovered the incredible secret to surviving amongst those unexpected struggles of, "Friendships, Family and Funerals." As sometimes when we don't see it, someone we love stays right by our side.

"Disappointments are a part of life. The most important thing you can do for your mate in a time of crisis is to love him or her. If your spouse's primary love language is physical touch, nothing is more important than holding her as she cries. Your words may mean little, but your physical touch will communicate that you care. Crises provide a unique opportunity for expressing love. Your tender touches will be remembered long after the crisis has passed. Your failure to touch may never be forgotten."

~ Gary Chapman

# IN LOVING MEMORY OF MICHAEL STEVEN TORRES, USMC

JUNE 8, 1983 – JULY 5, 2004

"What do you want to be little Michael?"
The first grade teacher would ask in surprise...
"To be a REAL HERO, just like my Dad" –
And his eyes would grow wide with pride.
Here, Michael's Dad would as well have a "calling"
Leaving Texas when the kids were small,
But, even once holding his Physician degree –
His four children mattered, MOST OF ALL!
You see, Dad and Michael would sometimes have struggles
And wouldn't always see things the same...
Yet, before his High School Graduation arrived,
They made time for sheer fun and some games.
So, they lived, they loved, they laughed again,
As though they had never been apart,
By computers, airplanes, calls and more...
While real forgiveness ruled their hearts.
Foremost through the years as Michael grew,
His long-term wish was still etched in his mind.
Then, this "first grader turned fearless" traded in college life,
For a destined ticket to Iraqi frontlines.
Therefore, it is by no mistake he'd return to us
Around Dad's birthday and our country's too...
For this trooper will be, forever-admiring them both,
Like he had so loved as a child to do!
Now, he's left behind Colonel Torres,
Who taught his boy to Aim High for his dreams -
While "Doc" proudly escorts our REAL HERO back,

As one of The Few, The Proud, The Marines!
Throughout this ordeal it occurred to me,
EACH OF US now has a job to do –
We must carry on
where Lance Corporal Torres left off,
Wrapped in THE RED, THE WHITE and THE BLUE!
Please let this battle-scarred awakening
Be THAT CHANCE to jump-start our own lives,
By reaching out to those we've been blessed,
Like our kids, ourselves our wives.
For the time has come for young and old
TO RISK, TO DANCE TO SING
As we too, resurrect our first grade dreams
Above all, LET FREEDOM RING!
For more than God needed a Soldier
He's taken a wonder he knew he could trust…
To now stand "On Guard" at Heaven's Gate
And welcome each of us!
So, if at times you are missing young Michael,
And feel tears misting up in your eyes…
You can always stay in touch with him
Simply turn, and SALUTE THE SKY!

**SADLY MISSED BY FAMILY, FRIENDS
AND FELLOW AMERICANS!**

"In Grateful Memory of Michael Torres, USMC. Gone but not forgotten."

In Honor of their real "Hometown Hero" - Michael's street signs today in El Paso, Texas.

*** As both an avid Cinderella collector and willful shoe-selling Goddess over the years (and always convinced there's still a part of me since childhood, who will joyfully be "part princess"), it seems perfectly fitting to add right here - the relative wording from one of my most-cherished Christmas ornaments complete with gold glitter, a crown and a small, dangling shoe below:

"The right shoe could change your Life …
just ask Cinderella."

# YET "ANOTHER MICHAEL'S" MAGIC

It never ceases to amaze me as I write on these truly sacred journeys that God continues to send people my way! Such would be the case, with my suddenly sent-from-another location, "Naturalizer Store Manager," Michael Korabek. Where, at first it may have seemed like he was only there for the expanding gap between some last-minute glitches with both surgeries and staffing, it became very clear almost overnight - that this calm, considerate and Christian man would teach me so much more. Moreover, I also knew, since successfully penning my *Life Is How YOU Look At It*, that it has "truly been the men named Michael" (like that of my learned-of Guardian angel's) –who amid their own miracle-filled awakenings, so keep on touching my life. And, this Michael would be no exception, as he one day shared the following etched forever-in-faith-first tale:

You see, years ago when Mike was a fifth grader, his family of four's house had sadly burned down. This was, only after beginning at the foot of his sister's bed, who was also a very sound sleeper. Though, as his father tried to put the fire out, he then fell and hurt his knee. Yet, more than anything this foursome savored, the fact that sweetly they were all safe. Meanwhile his very special grandfather had passed away only about three weeks earlier - leading this spiritual family to feel solidly like, he had "so angelically wherever he was at now," managed to wake his granddaughter up. Moreover, this really comforting thought also allowed Mike's mother to then peacefully let go of the heart-wrenching pain of recently losing her father to heaven. Likewise, amongst this so-surreal event also remained the reality, that most of their once-thought-needed possessions were heavily burned or had very serious water damage. But, even more amazing was the fact that one of the only articles to left to survive in one piece, was a single, potential church-supporting lottery ticket complete with some charring on the sides. Therefore, after ultimately needing to rent an apartment for sheltering both their coping and close-knit family, Mike's mom kept nixing the idea of purchasing it, while his Dad was both persistently and patiently pursuing her to do so even as their finances were now more-than-tight. Yet, a believing dad finally got his wish, when Mike's mom agreed one day to willingly spend the one-hundred dollars and therefore buy the ticket - and delightfully knew more than anything now, that God definitely provides for His trusting people when they took home the ten-thousand dollar prize!

Then, six months later, Mike's family would move back in their house as both finished being gutted and then finally repaired. When, about two weeks into their homecoming they would sadly suffer another loss. As somehow, a group of menacing kids had been patrolling their neighborhood, pretending to look for a hose. Meanwhile, as another neighbor had tried to address their antics, she was told gruffly to "Get back in the house!" Where next, it would be here, that Michael's unsuspecting family's garage would now get set on fire - and should it have freely burned about fifteen minutes longer, it would have once again destroyed their structure's already melting siding.

Though the biggest thing I've learned from the Korabek's is to stand united as a family, since nothing we'll ever go through remains stronger, than the sheer will of Grace and Faith! Lastly as my Shoe

Store Manager Mike, finished up his awesome story, between our "usual sorting of the sneakers and the stylish" – his truly been-there-done-that smile, has taught me to solidly believe, that in any situation God is always in control. After all, it truly was only a few years ago, where his cherished parents would also attend another church's annual festival – and again gratefully bring home from this divine parish as well, another ten thousand dollar prize!

> "But this I say: He who sows sparingly will also reap sparingly, and he who sows bountifully will also reap bountifully. So let each one give as he purposes in his heart, not grudgingly or of necessity; for God loves a cheerful giver."
>
> 2 Corinthians 9: 6-7
> "NKJV™"

"...Have you ever noticed that in a restaurant, you can almost always tell the difference between a dating couple and a married couple? Dating couples look at each other and talk. Married couples sit there and gaze around the restaurant. You'd think they went there to eat!"

~ Gary Chapman

## MY BIGGEST PET PEEVE

I think society today actually has an epidemic of those who've sadly traded their talk time for texting, the remote control for romance and are so busy hoarding all they have to ever help anyone out. Furthermore, even our young children don't seem to go anywhere in public without a bunch of electronic gadgets – while we were all forced as kids (from the Flintstone era!) to just boringly behave in public, or get our parent's dirty looks. Meanwhile, have you ever witnessed as I have, three teenagers walking down the street amid their obvious silence, though each texting all the way? Then, did you ever wonder as well: "Who could they all possibly be talking to?" And, whatever happened to that old one-on-one, of sweet communication amongst singing loudly around both the very warm and weekly bonfire, "Carry on (My) Wayward Son?"

Around the same time of pondering the above thoughts also, I would be walking by the television one night only to hear Oprah Winfrey herself, recommending a book entitled, *The 5 Love Languages* by Gary Chapman. And, while it's purple cover was already "a sure sign" that I should dig a little deeper, I was totally unprepared for the nurturing, and real awakening I'd awesomely receive next.

After all, as this successful author would then let us know amidst "some truly sparkling examples" – how our love relationships will ultimately keep on failing, unless we learn to communicate again with our cherished partners in ways that THEY understand. Yet, even with this wisdom in tow, I still found myself struggling most with my own primary and secondary needs now established from doing Gary's survey, of requiring both "physical touch and quality time." Especially since, as a young preemie I once stayed in an incubator for months- this newly-unveiled concept has become truly a comforting necessity for my well-being, not considered needy as I've been told. Couple this, also with the fact, that no one at my home really talked anymore, I couldn't help but see that, those "uninvesting-in-the-moment teenagers"- were actually mirroring something I missed! Moreover, as my Poppy would always say: "Be with someone you love to talk to Missy, as some year this may be all that you've got left," I more than understood. But, this reality didn't make it any easier once noticing, that many "public pleasing people" would rather text others endlessly (on silent) and watch reruns on TV - then to turn their energies inward towards their regularly-neglected partners, to optimally recreate the benefits of going from really lackluster to a Life overflowing with Love! Where, in regards to the above surely unexpected "light-bulb moment" amid my many suppressed tears, Gary Chapman also notably states in his enlightening pages regarding the treasured subject of quality time:

"By 'quality time' I mean giving someone your undivided attention. I don't mean sitting on the couch watching television together. When you spend time that way, ABC or NBC has your attention - not your spouse. What I mean is sitting on the couch with the TV off, looking at each other and talking, giving each other your undivided attention…

When I sit with my wife and give her twenty minutes of my undivided attention and she does the same for me, we are giving each other twenty minutes of life. We will never have those twenty minutes again; we are giving our lives to each other. It is a powerful emotional communicator of love."

\*\*\* Nancy's notes:

Though, more than anything here, I can't help but wonder, "Wouldn't twenty minutes a day be a really worthwhile investment towards mindfully breaking our growing population's negative cycle of: first, treating those nearest-and-dearest foremost, just like amoebas on some agendas – and then, unhealthily moving onward in our relationships from the ex onto the next?"

"I keep my heart and my soul and my spirit open to miracles."

~ Patrick Swayze

# A TRUE INSPIRATION TO ALL

(This story contains my "Sixth Special Sparkler" in the likes of my Hometown Hero below.)

    If there's one thing I can be sure of, my accountant, Randy Giannini is as helpful as he's a hero, amid being a man of his word. As each time I have brought this "truly gifted gentleman" my yearly income taxes to nervously be processed, he continues to make me proud. That is, of both his sharpened skills and his sparkling success! Though if truth be told, people always look at me a little funny when I share that my accountant is blind. Yet, Randy's true finesse for loving to crunch numbers and living out a life of courage was part of a vibrantly stellar vision that began some years ago.
    You see, during Randy's first job while in high school he worked at a local plant, where he "helped to unload the large drums that were sealed with lots of chemicals carefully stored inside." Though here also, he would witness firsthand, some very unfortunate incidents that only after ultimately "seeing was believing" - caused him to do an about-face and surely change his path. First off, as those big tractor trailer trucks would always pull up to be unloaded, he saw how one's safety latch's handle that should have secured its heavy contents, did unexpectedly jolt free from its position and break the jaw of a coworker's face. Next, Randy would than bear witness to observing a caustic line snap abruptly that would land on another

employee's shoulder causing severe burns to this man as well. Then sadly, when a chlorine gas leak then exploded all down the same street and blew off three very heavy manhole covers – he was not only counting his blessings, but amongst the heightened dangers that this work presented and his history of Juvenile Diabetes would decide on pursuing college instead.

Now, amidst his studies Randy earned a four year degree in Accounting, where he focused most on Corporate, Sales and Payroll taxes. Where, after graduation, he was then employed at a well-known bank, and later became a Comptroller of a company where he really needed to clean things up. At the same time, he now tells me as he utmost smiles very broadly, how "all his jobs since then have been related to nothing but taxes." Also, no matter what he was doing full time, he always did small business and personal returns for many clients on the side. But more than anything, his compassionate heart yearned to open an Accounting business - to not only focus more on his very cherished customers, but to finally branch out as well his instilled knack for crunching numbers foremost on his own.

In 1979, Randy married his first wife, where they next had two young children. Here too, this frequent athlete also kept himself really busy with the love of all his sports. Moreover, while now surprisingly informed that he was surely going to go blind someday, he kept up his promise of staying active - and was known to even play some solid Basketball as much as five days a week. Then, after several unsuccessful surgeries, including the one that was thought to be the "cure-all" for his dwindling vision, this usually upbeat accountant was left sightless, at the early age of only twenty nine. Though, the one thing Randy's larger-than-life heart, still has a very hard time accepting, is that he was able to lay eyes upon his first child, a son, though his vision had sadly languished just days before he would be able to both hold and hear his newborn girl.

Even more amazing to me, is how Randy Giannini has refused let this major obstacle stop him, as many people (including me!) would never have known amongst such obvious warmth and sensitivity that

I was dealing with someone blind. That was, until I would go into his office with my yearly taxes - as a young single mom with usually far more bills than bankroll that really needed his expertise. Though, it was here also, that I would get to know "the real Randy" along with each of his seeing-eye dogs, who over the years have helped him to still be able to work his sparkling magic. Where today as well, I'd be the first to tell you – you can always count on him. Since mindfully, every time that a new income tax season would fall upon us, Randy would bravely merge himself with my messy pile of papers and instantly put my mind at ease. Yet, more than anything during these appointments, I've so loved to catch up on "our truly parallel-at-times stories" – as always being such a treasured combination of cherished positives, pals and parenthood be they struggles or success.

On one such occasion, Randy and I talked about my how my daughter Beth (amidst always wanting to live right by our Poppy), was told by some of the other kids within in her ninth grade honors classes – that they "never would have guessed by her trendy stuff and the way she sparkled that she came from a trailer park." But, it was here too, that my youngest cherub would hold her head high, as she knew that we were doing our best to both keep her in the school she loved and also scholarship-bound. (After all, who else do you know as a student that had a 104 average in Latin, amid truly never forgetting the awesome wonders of her still favorite teacher today?) Though it was at this point also, that I would so vulnerably share with Randy, how "even after my older child, Michelle had moved out foremost from our mobile home, in her seemingly embarrassment – I still hoped with all my heart that my youngest would fit in." Meanwhile, I forever heard as well, some of my "very determined doctors always chirping in my ear how much I really needed to move out A.S.A.P." because (in their minds): "Trailer parks are full of only drugs and dirt bags, and the finest of guns and grief." Yet, in looking back now, I never realized how by emotionally getting real with this very-nagging worry while spending time with Randy was going to change my life. Since at this point, my very special accountant would next share with me a truly remarkable story, that would keep me, any time I even thought of it so INSPIRED to design my dreams. As in all honesty, it's not where you live but how you live, that allows one to spiritually attract also, those huge, life-altering miracles and become a blessing to another's heart! Here too, Randy would reflect back to a "from-way-back-in-his-high-school-day's account" regarding one of his best friends, Tom. Where, just like my daughters and I each did for a while, he grew up in a mobile home. Though, as time progressed Tom received a two-year degree from our local community college in Computer Software Design. Then, shortly thereafter he partnered with another friend and they began to subcontract their much demanded know-how at companies across the board. That was, until Tom's friend sold him back his portion, and then he progressed along alone. Where today, both Tom's "college expertise and that computer-related vision," have left him rolling in the dough. As miraculously also, he has since purchased a beautiful house in Florida, retired in his early forties and is a millionaire to boot. Meanwhile, as I must have heard sweet Randy reassuringly tell me over the years at least twenty humble times –"No matter what worldly goods Tom has today, he says that he could always return here to his roots and move back into that mobile home." Lastly, while this truly warm-fuzzy life lesson would always be the one to instantly restore my smile, it also illustrates perfectly how, sometimes others' so inspiring stories keep that sparkle alive in our hearts!

## A TRUE INSPIRATION TO ALL – PART II

Moreover, over the years Randy would always tell me yearly that amidst Bethany's "up-and-coming college with an M.B.A, in Accounting focus," that he would both surely take her on as an intern and optimally under his wing. And, when that time finally arrived, our so-supportive Randy again held true to his word. As each summer morning while Bethany headed off to his financially-based business with a real spring in her step, she so liked what she was learning to do! On the other hand, anytime I stopped in to so rarely to see her, I would find my daughter sitting behind her desk with always piles of files in tow. Then, as each shift would end Beth would return home to say how much she enjoyed going to Randy's family-oriented office, especially "because he always bought them all lunch." So, it is here, that I must totally confess that as "her-surely-not-there-very-often mother" and while only observing from the sidelines, believed wholeheartedly that my smallest was only absorbing some real Accounting basics and being spoiled with good food as well. Though, it would be down the road in Grad School that I'd so humorously learn the truth. Since delightfully here, with Randy's genuine guidance my own baby girl not only became an asset at balancing others' books right down to the penny, but was also the only student in one of her hardest classes to ace, a several-hours long financial scenario – where she needed to show her numerical answers each and every step of the way. Therefore, it was now very obvious to me also, that Randy Giannini's always-angelic assistance (even amid all the egg on my face) had given my daughter as well quite the gift!

Yet, happily through the years, even without his star-filled eyesight, Randy continues to remain both well-rounded and family-focused. Where still today, he works hard alongside his sweet office assistant, who "types everything while he talks." All this, after remarkably trading in his once, so less-enjoyed talking computer for a real human with a heart. Likewise, he still stays in shape by passionately pursuing his love of most sports - something he states "would never have been possible without some of his friends surely having his back." As even after going blind he has continued to pursue his passions – and has been known to still run races, play golf and even attended some of our local, Buffalo Bills' football games with a radio right by his side. Where positively too, in regards to the above thought process about his "continued participation always amidst some really treasured friends", I ultimately noticed the magnificence of this stellar reality being wondrously mirrored in a plaque that's always been hanging, on one of his main office walls. Since many years ago when I entered Randy's comfortable office at tax time – I couldn't help but question the history behind this "totally Olympic-themed pic." Then, naturally at this time, my hometown hero would explain that this photo had been taken during the summer of 1996 - where several area citizens had been nominated by others also, to propel the Olympic torch's travel through our city of Niagara Falls. Where excitedly now, this fun-loving man known as well, for wearing a red t-shirt at times boldly labeled with the words "blind runner," would be no exception here. Incredibly too, while carefully being attached to a friend's wrist also, with a coiled-filled like phone cord, a dependable Lou made sure that Randy wouldn't stumble, and solidly stuck beside him as he realized his big dream. That same, "about a quarter-of-a-mile-each trek" that had another nominated jogger running right past his successful accounting business! Though here also, we two would then giggle over the merging of our mindsets since we both knew that whether we'd each been freely running or religiously writing a book we were unable to take full credit. As blissfully, behind every wish-filled journey are those "You-should-seriously-go-for-it angels" willing to lend a hand! Yet, more recently while discussing this supportive scenario, Randy notes that "although at least I was able to thank my believers"- it would truly bother him wholeheartedly, when "whenever he'd cross a finish line his certainly 'while-blind feat' would move to the front and center", while his attached-at-the-wrist accomplice would only get ignored. And, while he still sums up today, how this repeated event would always make him really sad amidst some media exposure, may we each humbly remember always - that in order to truly S.P.A.R.K.L.E., we must also acknowledge both the wonder of our own answered prayers and the tireless, behind-the-scenes talent that helped us to achieve our goals!

    Meanwhile, never was Randy's tax help more valuable than after I had so-blindly written my own spiritually-guided first book, entitled *Life Is How You Look At It* late last year. Ironically, at this juncture I'd also endured some very big changes, like foremost losing my youngest daughter now primarily as an exemption for this mom on her own to claim. Furthermore, while now age twenty-something Beth, would also routinely "hag me" to save all my receipts just like I did to her with all her high school homework – I couldn't help but feel that my late Poppy and his ongoing vision of my own, now fulfilled, "sacredly-propelled purpose", would be so very proud. Where somehow next, even as the heightened fear of foremost losing my shirt big-time, was trying to move into the forefront, I knew the Lord would surely more-than-faithfully accompany me along too. So, as no surprise to sabotage, with all my year-long purchases and papers now neatly taped within my ledger, this tax appointment was also the day that our local snow plows were working overtime, to quickly move the mounds of snow squalls onto some really monstrous drifts. Besides, this wintry scene would not allow me either to drive my own car to Randy's, and since the parking curbside anywhere was totally impossible, I settled just for being basically dumped at the door. Where, for many days as well, I had previously promised myself "not to chicken out" before I'd heard my accountant's final tally. Furthermore, the soothing Bible verse from Psalm 46:10 "Be still, and know that I am God" had been stuck in my head for weeks! So, instead of getting all worked up like a fidgety little kid about to get a shot at my pediatrician's - I instead chose not to panic, and next felt the most "surrealist blanket of Almighty Peace" permeate the room. Then, about thirty minutes later, and right before Randy would next figure my final totals, he would now ask me one last time if all my book writing extras and expenses had been included across the board. So suddenly, I flipped again through my properly organized ledger as requested, only to reveal a forgotten page. As somehow, those "plastic purple bags" that I had so stressfully ordered, late last year right around my birthday for my upcoming book signings - would not only get last-minute added in here, but would become my saving grace. Incredibly as well, just when Randy's treasured assistant would finally enter my just "Let go and let God totals" – I knew that true miracles still exist. Where to my delight, my total taxes owed both to the State and divinely refunded by Federal, even after all my book's publishing, promoting and purple bag costs amid some bouts of real perseverance - were less than fifty bucks!

Finally, it never ceases to amaze me that no matter what Randy Giannini is going through he continues to focus gratefully, upon the promising plus side of life. More recently also, as I was prayerfully meditating one morning, on the theme for this next, very precious (and purple!) book, I was sacredly told to "showcase my own Seven Special Sparklers" - who'd helped most lead my healing journey joyously into the light. And, while this colorful vision continued to unfold with answers, about manifesting my vibrant seven's stories, my inspiring accountant who just refuses to cease having visions, came instantly first to mind. Where, even today, as Randy has since "lost his beautiful second wife, Linda," to a courageous bout with cancer – he somehow continues to remain upbeat. After all, he says, "Although I get depressed sometimes on the inside, I try not to let it show. I'm alive and well. I could be worse off. I just have to make the most of the senses I have left. I don't feel blind, but prefer to count my blessings." he says, amid his trademark smile – making the resilient Randy I know a real beacon in keeping this world a brighter place!

> "I found that the things that hurt us the most can become the fuel and the catalyst that propel us toward our destiny. It will either make you bitter or it will make you better."
>
> ~ T.D. Jakes

Randy Giannini (taken in the late 1990's),
The bravest "blind runner" I know!

"There are always going to be dark times we wish that we could avoid or erase from our lives. But our dark times show us our light and our strength. They make us who we are today. Good or bad they are all meant to help us shine."

~ Jennifer Gayle

## I KNOW WHAT IT'S LIKE ...

I know what it's like to think that a partner
Was the best thing that I'd ever had,
Until I remembered those million-sung lyrics
To "Two Out of Three Ain't Bad."
I know what it's like to work holidays past,
For extra pay and just not to be home,
Yet, by now knowing the real meaning of Christmas
Means that I'll NEVER, again be alone.
I know what it's like to be repeatedly told I'm no good
And that "my gifts" aren't truly ones I've been given,
To now taking the High Road as God continues His work
And molds my life into one that's worth livin'.
I know what it's like to preserve some Lord's time
And to have others laugh or get really upset,
Though, after being used as one of "his lighthouses"
He's forged a path I will never forget!
I know what it's like to have been around those
Who no longer send cards, gifts or flowers …
Amid taking any adversity aimed right at me
And surrendering it to a much Higher Power!
I know what it's like to be told
That "I have nothing worth hearing,

Talk too fast and interrupt way too much,"
While being explicitly informed by Our Savior
"To just keep leading by humbled example"
To those who could use His tender touch.
I know what it's like to be sitting with someone
And feel totally "homeless" amid worlds apart,
While knowing with God coming first in my life,
He'll ALWAYS cherish and comfort my heart.
I know what it's like to have a real dislike
For others' lack of accountability or created drama–
Preferring instead, just to meditate or simply read a good book
While they save their antics for their own momma!
I know what it's like to beg God at my lowest
To send me "the light of a true Christian man,"
Who firmly supports both my calling to write, from the heart-
And will faithfully take my love-and-learn hand.
After all, it's been Christ Jesus who's since taught me
That people should each have a place in our life -
And, that dead-last is truly no place to put,
Your husband, your angel, your wife.
I also know what it's like to be ignored on my birthday,
And left home while big things are forgotten,
Until I prayerfully learned to celebrate daily
The awesome birth of His Child begotten!
I know what it's like to have lived beside someone
Usually grumpy and so very cold,
While wondering, "Who will take care of me?"
When, I'm foremost gray and old.
I know what it's like to love "being in love,"
From his smile, to his touch to his kiss,
Then, to have all this replaced in an instant
Making my "being heard" the most that I've missed.
I know what it's like to address with God's love
My past's pain and my wildest fears…

*S.P.A.R.K.L.E.*

While also being enlightened that: "When others
Keep pointing out what they dislike in us most"
We are actually being used as THEIR mirrors!
I know what it's like to think that things are good
Yet, to have the rug ripped right out underneath,
But, since trusting fully in the Lord's timing
I'll ALWAYS land back on my feet.
I know what it's like to have had my heart
Both majorly torn and tattered,
While hitting rock bottom taught me real quick,
What so totally truly matters!
I know what it's like to feel replaced in one's eyes
By someone else sitting in the very same room,
Amidst God's telling me to "divinely concentrate
Most on my need to S.P.A.R.K.L.E." -
And dispel Satan's worldly gloom.
As, it's not our many possessions,
Or those funds that we keep in the bank,
That can match that feeling of
Simply enjoying the present moment
Amongst so gratefully still giving thanks.
Because more than anything, my late Poppy taught me
"How the right man won't make me cry"…
Yet, when one wondrously lifts up their will to the Lord,
A huge part of what was surely dies.
Since you too, will find yourself much less tolerable
Of those who act like "real porcupines" –
While trying so hard "to needle their negatives
Right under your skin"…
With their woes, their wants and their whines!
But, here also you needn't worry
Because on a way more positive note,
While you make time to mindfully rest and relax
They'll leach onto others who might help them cope.

So, please don't let bitterness, hoarding and distancing
Define your free-will of actions today,
As in the light of God's pending judgment
We'll all answer foremost someday.
You see, by becoming a Born-again Christian,
As though being rushed, under really brisk water –
I've uncovered the unconditional thrill of being,
One of the Lord's victim-to-very-blessed daughters!
Where those days of both loving and losing big-time
Have unveiled also my spiritual niche,
Making those times I'd endured only turbulence and thorns
Seriously now, the ones I wouldn't switch.
As maybe, life is meant to be less about
Whether we're liked, or thin or wealthy …
Which, then allows us to attract way more,
Situations that are healthy.
Meanwhile, each and every time I watch the magic
As one of my "so-surreal journey's doors" suddenly closes…
I'm surely in awe as I'm still sent cherished signs,
Like the brightest of rainbows and roses!
After all, when I'm truly quiet and make time to listen,
I can hear God's healing voice so much more,
Though, I don't always know where I'm heading
I've told Him "Please take me, I am yours."
I've also realized, that the people who are the most envious of us
Seem to sabotage our grace-filled successes the most,
Until I discovered the bliss of real "triple love" -
In the Father, Son and His Holy Ghost!
Then, I learned what it's like to cast my cares
And to always remember to "Focus on Up"
Amid appreciating more of the basics I own
After giving away lots of my stuff.
So today, as others still remain very busy
Keeping score of my "many blunders"-

My God so faithfully keeps illuminating my path,
With His word, His grace and His wonders!
To now knowing whatever He's planned for me
Certainly couldn't be any worse,
I'll hold tight to His vibrance and verses
Like gold coins within my purse.
So make magic, make memories
Make each moment count -
By making sweet, angelic guidance
What you can't live without.
Where in closing, I know there's always going to be
A real abundance of hope for tomorrow,
When we freely hand over our hearts to the Lord
And trade S.P.A.R.K.L.I.N.G. for our many sorrows!

> "The Scripture teaches that we have a valuable treasure on the inside. You have a gift. You have something to offer that nobody else has. You didn't just show up on planet Earth by accident. You were handpicked by Almighty God. He saw you before you were formed in your mother's womb and placed you here for a reason. You have an assignment. There's something that God wants you to accomplish. Somebody needs your touch. Somebody needs what you have.
>
> Don't live with this treasure undiscovered, and don't die with that treasure still in you. Press forward. Give birth to the dreams and desires that God has placed in your heart."
>
> ~ Joel Osteen

"Have the courage to follow your heart and intuition. They somehow already know what you truly want to become."

~ Steve Jobs

# THE DAY THE GOSLING GOT LET GO

About five years after I'd met "Lucy," my colorfully psychic stepmom, she delightfully called me one day, seemingly out of the blue. While, this was not like our usual calls to just finally catch up – she shared something so insightful, that I still think about it today! As there really is tons of truth to the fact that "others become our magic mirrors" – while spiritually coming on the strongest amidst those subjects that we need to work on the most. Since, on this very sunny fall day, sweet Lucy would explain about how an incredible scenario she'd just witnessed was still very much stuck in her head. You see, across the street from her country-bumpkin farm house (that still contains my old umbrella!), was a field covered in both colorful weeds and wilting cornstalks. Where, upon sipping some warm tea upon her soft wind and wicker-filled patio, she ultimately caught a glimpse of such a precious rite of passage. As here, while she watched in amazement, a real-life "Mother Goose" would heartwarmingly be teaching her four busy, little goslings about how to cross the street. Yet, as Lucy celebrated from the sidelines, she couldn't help but notice how only three of these four cheered-on offspring had successfully made the trek. Then, upon squinting further across the way near all the cornstalks and camouflage-sat one small baby gosling, totally shaking in its shoes. Moreover, this sacred moment of reflection, showed my always-supportive stepmom, that although she technically now had "four kids" amidst my treasured presence, it was time to let one go. And, without blinking an eye, an intuitive-also

Lucy, would explicitly know – how this trembling little gosling that had so-prospered in her presence was no one else but me!

Yet, throughout the years, that special analogy of how gentle, nudging Lucy "truly, taught me (once so nervously like a child again!) to optimally 'skate' with confidence – has set the stage for my true calling. Especially as I now humbly focus on being a purpose-driven adult – this triumph has continued to aid my courage to move eternally forward, while walking in God's with-me grace.

Though, in saying goodbye to Lucy's really steadfast support, I also found myself reflecting upon those many wonderful times we had, whether we were both learning to grow graciously amongst warm brownies or even grappling with our grief. When, suddenly I was reminded of "the biggest laugh-out-loud moment," that we'd ever shared in our lives. After all, as she also once dared me to include this, truly hilarious story in the pages of one of my projects – it also does prove perfectly as well, as my late Poppy so endlessly tried to teach me, to ALWAYS come prepared. As it was he, once headed home to heaven, who still managed to prove his point that: "I should always carry a flashlight"- from my purse to my red Pontiac, just in case there was a need. Therefore once he'd actually passed on, and from the pages of my previously-written *Life is How YOU Look At It*, I'd unexpectedly become the lucky owner of "his unwanted by the others' things." These were items like his Mickey Mouse pancake griddle, that fully-stocked, aqua crocheted toilet paper doll to always have a surplus - and a plastic flashlight with some working batteries to boot! Where, as no surprise to either of us, it would be ME surely finding myself in such a side-splitting dilemma- as what better place to experience a power failure, then in the Gynecologist's office for a yearly (and no generator truly available) with my feet up in the stirrups? So, even then, as I really did need to reschedule my appointment for a more illuminated visit, Lucy also always kept on so-humorously pointing out how: "I couldn't even go for a basic pap smear without a blessed power failure" – as optimally too, every time we two would even think of this little… Let there be light bumble, we couldn't help but burst out and laugh!

"You may discover that, sometimes, if you don't keep things stirred up, God will stir things for you. When somebody leaves your life or a relationship is over- whether it is a business partner, a friend, a neighbor or a coworker who parts company-don't get upset. Don't try to talk them into staying. Let God do the new thing. Understand that your destiny is not tied to the people that walk away from you."

~ Joel Osteen

"One of the most beautiful gifts in the world is the gift of encouragement. When someone encourages you, that person helps you over a threshold you might otherwise never have crossed on your own."

~ John O'Donohue

# WHOSE LIFE HAVE YOU LEFT IMPRINTS ON?

Remarkably, it would be about four years later, when this "really grateful gosling" would surprisingly receive a letter from that leopard-loving step mom that I truly still adore. Where excitedly here, as I tore open the white envelope I found the following warmly enclosed:

"Hi Nanc,

How's your life going these days? I've been thinking about you a lot as I get ready to close my store and render it into good and caring hands. You were and still are the turning point in my life. It was you who gave me so much strength to keep going with the store. I felt like looking at you was like looking in a mirror (the same sentiment I'd expressed about her, in *Life Is How YOU Look At It*!) But I have to hand it to you... you are a lot stronger than I was at that time. You have mitzvah! You are the one that I use as an example for other woman who come into my store. You are the one who never says die. You are a part of what every lost soul should be... strength! You teach and you learn. I love you! I'm sitting here in my kitchen, having a cup of tea and thinking of you. I will always think of you because you gave me the tea caddy and I use it every day ... :}. I have a cup of Nanc every day... hahahaaaha. You will always be the most memorable person to ever come in my store. For that I am grateful. People have come into my store and left (I guess that karma's been paid) but you've stayed in my life and have become a very important part of my family and myself. We all need some of your feisty spiritedness from time to time. I hope you got the store update I sent out, and will feel free to stop at the house whenever you can. Maybe now that I'll be having some free time to myself, WE CAN DO LUNCH!!! Do ya think?

Just wanted to let you know… I love you!"

Lucy

\*\*\* For my Cherished Readers,

In regards to this story, here is another sparkling thought for your spirit to consider:

"A blessed life is all about willfully learning to live – as we'll never know our inner sparkle's realm, until we really learn how to give."

# EACH OF US HAS A DREAM...

Deep within our hearts,
each of us carries the seed
of a secret dream,
special and unique to each individual.
Sometimes another person
can share that dream
and help it grow to fulfillment;
other times, the dream remains
a solitary pursuit, known only to
the seeker. But secret or shared,
no matter what it might be, a dream is a
potential which should never be discouraged.
For each of us also carries within ourselves
a light which can cause the seed
to grow and blossom
into beautiful reality...
that same light I've seen shine
so clearly in you.

~ Edmund O'Neill

The poem "Each of us has a dream..." by Edmund O'Neill is from the Blue Mountain Arts book Always *Follow Your Dreams, Wherever They Lead You*. Copyright © 2001 by Blue Mountain Arts, Inc. Reprinted by permission. All rights reserved.

"The positive thinker sees the invisible, feels the intangible and achieves the impossible."

~ Anonymous

# SOME REAL SUPPORT OF STEEL

(*** This story contains my "Seventh Special Sparkler" in the so-spirited, Nik Wallenda.)

Needless to say, right before the start of summer 2012, my life was somewhat of a mess. Yet, in this very same week, I'd just prayerfully submitted my (thought-to-be) final draft of *Life Is How YOU Look At It* to my publisher, and then two days later, moved out amidst a bunch of little, baby steps - to a very peaceful apartment after leaving Allen's antics behind. And, while he was less-than-thrilled that I'd left him, I planned to exit what at times, largely felt like boot camp and basically never look back. Though sometimes, when we *think* that our choices are set in stone, God spiritually then has a say! Moreover, while I must have heard Joyce Meyer stress a thousand times, on her *Enjoying Everyday Life* radio show, something to the effect of: "When it comes to wishing others would change, only God changes His people," and that my efforts would be better spent surrendering this uphill issue, and ultimately working on myself. At the same time, I insightfully knew that I had managed to survive some other really relentless obstacles in my life by simply asking the Lord to take over the reins. Somehow too, I've learned, that this conscious surrender has always revealed, His such-stellar blessings being bestowed upon me. Like, those warm-fuzzy feelings I always get whenever I spread His Love, to so gratefully being able to speak in tongues, whenever

I seriously need to pray. At this time as well, I began rereading many books including Jill Kelly's, *Without a Word How a Boy's Unspoken Love Changed Everything* and saw a wondrously shining example within, that only God's Divine Intervention allows for anyone's true brokenness to become incredibly whole again.

Though here, nothing could have prepared me for the call I'd receive next. After all, Allen had so-pompously already visited my favorite couple's house, after telling them also something like: "If he had been truly happy with me, he would have never turned outward from us." Then, he left town to enjoy a forty-something birthday weekend with his, always-have-time-for "importants" - making it so much easier for me to just willfully close the door. Yet, the very next morning would begin with a call from one of my little loves, saying that Allen had called her sobbing, as he had been previously hoping to both, "come clean to me over this exact birthday weekend about his wayward happenings" and also pledge more to help with my bills. Though instead, his own illuminating magic mirror showed that due to his true insensitivity and botched priorities he'd surely lost as he next shared sadly – the best thing of his life. And, while this was truly a miracle-in-the-making to see my long-lost Romeo's heart resurface, it was then, that I, would surprisingly receive his many text messages stating things like: "Please come home to a man who needs you", and "I'd like to take you out on a date." Meanwhile, I was still very much overwhelmed by the landslide I had been left dodging, and decided instead of making a major split-second decision, I would concentrate on trying to seriously forgive him while letting the Lord's will chart my course.

Then, the very next night, I would be lying in bed (which also now was the evening of his birthday), when I couldn't help but wonder: "What HAD ultimately happened to Allen, to make him want old 'boring me' back?" Furthermore, when he called me that night I actually answered, only to find out something so amazing it could only be Our Savior's work! As here, Allen next explained, that when he'd returned home to his primarily empty house amid all the heightened pain without my presence – it was at this very lackluster moment that he stood tall within the living room and boldly asked God to reenter his life. Where also, if truth be told here, if I hadn't experienced the Holy Spirit's so-healing work within my own sparkle-free behavior – and surely amongst some others' truly shining examples placed before me, I never would have believed a single word of what he'd said. Where, as the story continues, the minute Allen foremost asked the Lord back into his world, a sudden feeling of "being struck by lightning actually pierced right through his body" – not only getting his act together, but landing him on the floor! Yet, ever-so-cautiously for me in all the hoopla, I was in no hurry to get hurt again.

Then, willfully that next week (after way more talks and tears), I agreed to meet Allen over at his house for just a simple meal. Furthermore, as I came prepared with our favorite Healthy Choice dinners, we also decided on having some scoops of his half-eaten Cookie Dough ice cream for dessert. Though, the thing that makes me "still smile most about that evening's surely basic preparations" was how also appearing at his nicely-set table, was a little, red stub of a lit candle sitting on a CorningWare dish – as being the only smidgeon of wax he said I'd somehow left behind, for him to humbly show he cared! But, I knew more than anything, amidst such obvious wings of brokenness we were going to need some God-guided work. Next, after supper, Allen requested that I walk with him down at Niagara Falls. And, while I knew how much this very sacred place had aided me through my painful times of real abandonment- I didn't know how therapeutic it might be in putting our shattered pieces, somehow back into place. I also knew that since my writing journey had sweetly blossomed there, and "the Lord always has my surrendered life load," I felt surely in light of all this insight, that I had nothing left to lose. So, on this day, June 14, 2012, Allen and I would get into his car and head down to my favorite spot amid the rainbows and the rocks. When delightfully too, between our attempts to talk amongst this really uphill challenge, we both realized, how it "would be only about twenty-four hours later," when Nik Wallenda, the high wire artist - would attempt to bravely cross via only a very narrow tightrope up and over both this slick and natural mist! All this, to be surreally accomplished without him somehow, "losing his steady focus" of making it safely to the other side. Where suddenly, as Allen and I so-comfortably walked and talked, we got increasingly close to the cordoned off fencing- to have something forever-impact my life. As it was here, that I would simply stretch up and touch Nik's surely fate-filled tightrope, and then I knew, from the slippery steel and the way it bobbled - how this feat would be majorly impossible (even with his deemed mandatory harness) - without some faithful backing from God. Moreover, this situation paralleled perfectly, how at times when we've each ultimately tried to reach for the stars, it didn't matter if we clumsily slipped or stumbled (while especially owning this behavior in our primary relationships) – because it takes such courage it takes such courage anyway, to ever passionately pursue our goals! Yet, this "wanna-do feat would wondrously become one very big exception"- as that very next night, Nik amid such abundant blessings and some surely stellar steps as shown on the Discovery Channel, would excitedly achieve this dream!

Then, please fast-forward to about one year later, as Mr.Wallenda had already successfully conquered with true wonder, the majestic makeup of Niagara Falls. When now, I found my eyes glued to the TV once again, while he would attempt to take on without a trusty harness and only his two-inch thick wire, the mighty Grand Canyon as well. Where mindfully next, as all of the viewing audience held our breath, he slowly inched over the little Colorado Gorge's splendor – where I was not only impressed with his wondrous footwork, but more with his non-stop faith! Since, there truly wasn't a time when Nik wasn't thanking both the Lord and his friends and family, for so-steadfastly supporting his trek. Yet, here also, I couldn't help but wonder, even as Allen and I continue to make some really small steps with God's help, in maybe restoring our relationship, "Why aren't all our cherished children exposed far more to this positive, prayer, pride and pledge to the flag behavior, instead of existing amidst some genuinely all-about-me-first-and-foremost 'adults' (from all walks of life!), who refuse to get along?"

"Keep yourself in a healthy physical environment. If you tend to struggle with discouragement and depression, don't sit around in a dark house all day long thinking about your problems. Open the windows; let the sun shine in. Put on some good uplifting music. Create a positive environment ... Find somebody happy to cheer you up. Get around people who will inspire you to rise higher. Be careful with whom you associate, especially when you feel emotionally vulnerable, because negative people can steal the dream right out of your heart."

~ Joel Osteen

# YOUR BIRTHDAY SHOULD BE BEAUTIFUL –

## THE LEGACY OF MY LABOR DAY LECTURE

> "How people treat you is their karma: how you react is yours."
>
> ~ Wayne Dyer

It was Labor Day weekend in 1977, and I decided to ride my bike over and catch up with Poppy, as somehow at the age of thirteen, I'd become too busy to stop by sooner. Yet little did I know, as I rehearsed my reasons for not making him matter, that he also had some matters to take up with me! As upon my arrival, I was shocked to discover a truly sad Ann Landers column entitled, "It Was Grandfather's Birthday" and an exasperated grandfather awaited – seemingly the lucky one out of eleven elusive-at-times grandchildren to be called on the carpet. Here too, like any other afternoon, Poppy loved to get his passionate point across. Where in many instances, he creatively counted on the wit and wisdom of "Annie Landers" (as he'd called her), while also leaving me to believe at this age, that they were more like close friends, than a faithfully reading ex-farmer with a flair for her finesse! Yet, unlike several times before when Poppy quoted from Ann's answers, this day would be much different making them both no match for me. Besides, when his rarely seen pout, combined with her easily recognized photograph, I immediately sensed that when these two teamed up together, I was headed for real trouble. Next, as Poppy laid his cards on the table I was right, as there was no disputing the cold hard facts. You see, only weeks earlier at the end of August, my excited grandfather had been patiently perched at his picnic table, to await our family's expected arrival, just like that grandfather did in his porch chair in Ann's now-so-cherished column. Here, Poppy next further explained in a quivering voice, how "with our sweet Grammie passed on only less than a year his freshly-forgotten birthday had hit harder than the rest," amidst faithfully figuring as well, that he could always count on his remaining relatives to help relieve his emptiness. Then, he continued on to convey the heartfelt hurt he'd experienced, just like the grandfather also in Annie's column, when not one of us old-enough-to-know-better grandkids took some time to celebrate his cause. Moreover, this was the first time I ever remember seeing (or regretfully making) Poppy cry – as this life lesson hit home like a boomerang to the back of my head! In the meantime, as tears ran down both of our faces, I not only ended up with a good case of "the guilt's" but was instantly enlightened to the fact that, people are precious and need to be noticed for the gifts that they are – not only on their birthdays but every day! So, while Poppy continued to air his woes, his words continued to echo with truth, while being sadly reinforced by his reality that; "You children all know Missy, where to turn for chauffeur service, cash up-front and even fresh cashews from the can in my cupboard!" Where next, not only had I been called on the carpet, but was feeling small enough to crawl right underneath it as Poppy's awful birthday analysis was seriously right on target. Besides, as threaded by tradition, he had ALWAYS remembered my birthday with wonderful cards pictured with my passions. From prima ballerinas, to poems and prayers, etched with pretty flowers, he'd kept track from the yellowing pages of his prized address book. Yet, more important than the three crisp dollar bills stuffed inside our envelope each year (until that sweet-sixteenth birthday cut off where sixteen special dollars eagerly awaited us), was the valuable life lesson Poppy patiently portrayed. Once showing me solidly how "one's birthday bliss should be less focused on the price tag of the present" and more about celebrating the special people in your life, the true meaning behind this memoir has brought more happiness to my heart than a house full of possessions ever could!

Thankfully too, once this Labor Day weekend's showdown of sadness subsided, I evolved into an adolescent with an unexpected awakening of putting people's feelings first. Moreover, after teaching me well to mindfully blow up in the moment, then magically let it blow over – I also learned that pent-up anger is most harmful to the hardened heart that chooses to harbor it. When shortly thereafter, my grandfather returned to his old softened self, as we next slurped sweetened strawberry sundaes in his aging honor. Here also, I was delighted to discover that semi-melted ice cream was totally therapeutic in soothing away that large lump in my throat. (Moreover, when looking back at this moment now, I'm still awestruck at how smart and successful a man he really was – as sometimes, no matter how hard someone tries to teach us something, it seriously doesn't sink in, until we find ourselves submerged in it). Then, once happily hugging Poppy goodbye, I was homebound on my bike, while never realizing at this time the profound effect his still stinging sermon would still have on my heartstrings today.

## YOUR BIRTHDAY SHOULD BE BEAUTIFUL - PART II

Remarkably in retrospect, when I reflect upon my childhood I have memories of only two birthday parties, one in cherished family photos and the other cautiously witnessed through a quivering child's eyes. You see, my first birthday was magically celebrated with relatives and friends amidst the taking of black-and-white pictures. Where here, while prettily pictured atop my tiny red tricycle (with two blocks of wood tightly taped to the pedals so I could easily reach my dangling destination), I was also accompanied by my newly-acquired playmate, Susie, as I cradled her along for the ride. After all, this special ragdoll was just gifted to me, by none other than my named-after, Aunt Nancy. Yet, somehow now the tables have turned- as it is me who now counts on the spirit of "Sweet Susie" to carry me through the tough times! Here too, I have uncovered another perfect example of while some things change others stay the same. Since today, I still require some help to reach my car's gas pedal, while forever needing to sit upon an old hardcover book that humorously fixes my field of vision up over the wipers of my white Jeep. And even now, as my girlfriends continue to find this use for an old encyclopedia far too amusing, I opt to celebrate the upside to this – as hopefully, by some form of osmosis its seemingly historical contents (especially after all those high school classes I'd skipped), may someday absorb through my tush!

Meanwhile, my other birthday "faded flashback," was from the tender age of first grade, and filled with far less-than-perfect memories. As on this day, while surrounded in celebration with both close friends and cherished classmates, I can primarily remember hearing my father's booming outburst from atop our basement stairs. Where foremost here, while yelling for all of us petite partygoers to either "settle down and be quiet or everyone would be going home" – he then to my further embarrassment shut off all the lights until we got his angry drift. In the meantime, I observed how it was much safer to stuff things inside "like a good girl should," then to casually let loose and live life to the fullest, and therefore alleviate the risk of repercussions from angering those I respected most. Likewise, also during these oldest daughter days I became terrified of the dark after being locked in our linen closet as a preschooler by my laughing, year-older neighbor. Where amid the shrill sound of police sirens he teasingly said further that: "The cops are coming to take you off to jail" while I trembled amongst all the towels. Positively though, since those times of being treated woefully as a prisoner I'm proud to say that I have since healed enough to welcome both the unique serenity of darkness and the uniformed sight of policeman (while also wondering why they don't have a boarding house for annoying big boys to stay at, until we someday begin to like them again!) But, fortunately too, while traveling back in my mind to that first-grade party fiasco, I became blessed with the steadfast belief – if you aren't supposed to have fun at your birthday bash, then where on Earth should you be allowed?

Some years later, it would again be Poppy's way of looking at life through his forgiving eyes of faith and fairness, which would seriously set me straight. Where, along with the gifted guidance of a great therapist, I was taught to assume full responsibility for my own satisfaction, while also comprehending also, that I only have myself to blame if I chose giving up grudgingly over growing up guilt-free. So, by sweetly substituting the blame game for being truest to my own feelings first, I undeniably began to replace failures with freedom and revealed my real risk-taking self! Then, by consciously surrendering my childhood scrapes and struggles (by "airing them out on the surface, instead of burying them under some Band-Aids soaked in the burning of Bactine") I quickly discovered that he only way to release our hurts are to: wholeheartedly feel them first, forgive those who seemed to inflict them second and lastly relinquish those previously painful pitfalls to rest peacefully in our past.

Then incredibly, during the first year after my more recent marital stress-fest, while also experiencing the wonders of the single mom one-step-up-and-twenty-back syndrome, I was in for quite another shock to my system. Since unfortunately here, I would once again be visited by the "Your Birthday Should Be Beautiful Boomerang," which had ultimately resurfaced to my regret. And, just like Poppy's experience, it would be my turn next to learn this life lesson the hard way, as my two daughters would be spending the overnight at their daddy's house, on my first birthday as fully free. While also setting a long-term goal to learn to like my loneliness, amid the new lifestyle we'd landed in – I felt strongly against making my kids stay home to become my "security blankets." Therefore instead, I decided they should remain steady with their weekly routine. Besides, I'd banked on the fact that my closest family and fan club of friends would be dropping by in droves – to celebrate both the filing of my newly-done divorce and upcoming November birthday, all with that sparkling finesse we were at times so famous for. Yet, to my dismay, the magic mirror of meltdowns threw a major monkey wrench in my direction as only a few sweet souls stopped for cake or even called to care, leaving me crumbled. Then, once I received a bag of much-needed socks with holes in the toes of two of the six pairs – this scenario became the critical straw that seriously broke the camel's back. Where next, I childishly crawled into bed at eight-thirty and then cried myself to sleep. Yet, from the height of real compassion, it truly was my cherished cousin's kindness that helped to tuck me in that night, as the heartbroken first grader I'd honestly regressed into. But truthfully, while hurting all over again from hopes gone haywire (that together she and I now laugh about today!) this scene proves perfectly, how most of our heart-wrenching situations don't revolve around what's seemingly bothering us in the present – but have way more to do with reliving those unhealed traumas that stem from triggers past.

On a more positive note, my next birthday would be blissfully better as I took some time to pre-plan my party. See, this year I eagerly invited five of my favorite girlfriends out to a restaurant in my homely-no-more honor, as my two daughters wouldn't be returning until later. Happily now, we gossiped and giggled (just like first graders again) amidst a memorable mix of laughter, love and long-term memories into evening's early hours. Then, once this enjoyable affair was over, I arrived home just in time to inhale a piece of Pepperidge Farm Coconut Layer Cake and some strawberry ice cream on the side with my favorite family foursome. Though above all, this sweet scenario seriously enlightened me that: "although at times, 'back-at-ya' burns - behind every negative catastrophe appears the chance to change our ways." Therefore, by responding with resilience, instead if retreating with regret – I'd lusciously learned to boomerang back on my own birthday with a four-star cause for celebration. Meanwhile, from this point on, I also affirmed that although some of my previous festivities were surely nightmares-in-the making, as the newfound owner of my outlook they no longer needed to be!

In all honesty though, the idea of creating a new treasury of birthday traditions had not originated from me this year, and had only crossed my path about three weeks earlier. Besides, as both my cherished Poppy and the crushed Grandfather in Annie's column had taught me, sometimes our empathy can only be expanded, by viewing life's truly pain-filled pathways through the eyes of the opposite side.

## YOUR BIRTHDAY SHOULD BE BEAUTIFUL – PART III

It was late one October afternoon and I was busy running ragged amidst a stack of endless errands. When suddenly, I found myself "stopped within my tracks" while waiting for the woman to slowly call my number, at the Social Security office. Since also knowing as well, that the Lord will never give me more tasks than I can handle, I took this screeching halt as a sign to stand still in the moment. Then next, as I luckily leafed through some reading material, I located a small piece of advice that I sweetly still practice today! Where, as the reader here, I was expressly advised on my upcoming birthday to purchase for myself a dozen red roses. Now, I was to simply send one of these tender blossoms to twelve truly special people, who'd totally touched my life. Here, it was also suggested to include a message something similar to the following footnote: "Today is my birthday. Thank you for being one of my greatest gifts." In the meantime, I closed my eyes while lost in thought, and began to meditate on this magical mission. Where before long, I felt a familiar wave of warmth rush over me, all-the-while-knowing I'd stumbled onto something big! Blissfully too, as I envisioned myself putting this "Your Birthday Should Be Beautiful" wisdom into play, I was awestruck by an amazing thought! By fully focusing on the individual intricacies that each single rose exuded, along with taking the time to examine the overall beauty of the bunch – I too, felt beyond blessed. As this enlightening concept continued to highlight just how cherished my own collection of "friendship flowers" really is, both in those memorable moments full of fun or full of fertilizer. Excitedly, as I gave names to the owners of these dear-to-me dozen, they represented both a precious mix of never-deserting pals and newly-discovered people. Yet above all, I couldn't help but ponder the magnitude of this serene, fun floral fantasy. Moreover, while being such a wonderful way to send others some serious sunshine, really, since when do we as heart-beating humans think to give out instead of get back on our birthdays? Then naturally now, my tears would begin to flow as these gifted guidelines appeared right before my eyes just when I really needed to read them. To my further credit, the heartbreak I had experienced during my childhood bygone birthdays, could no longer cast a shadow upon the babe that I'd become. Furthermore, by easily exchanging pity parties for "Diva dinners with some of my favorite petals" I've uncovered that Life Lessons are less importantly learned and more importantly lived.

Thankfully also, I'm happy to reveal that since that September 1977 Labor Day lecture, I never did forget Poppy's birthday again – while treasuring our time even more with cute cards, cherished phone calls and even his favorite, custard cream puffs! Yet, even as our Grandfather's will to go on daily began to woefully diminish – our entire clan still clustered to celebrate his upcoming day. (Here too, I can't help but smile as I reminisce about a time when my own two girls were small and we were watching a cartoon video together. At this time, we learned all about "un-birthdays" which is any day pin-pointed on the calendar to celebrate someone's birthday just because – as our journey should be more about holding our loved ones dear, than having their party on the right date. Humorously too, I found this thought to be quite an interesting concept, as my kids still giggle over the frostbitten fact about how in the "olden days" – I could never have hosted a pool party for my gal pals in November!

As mentioned earlier, Poppy aimed to treat us all equally. Therefore, not even summer hospice-care-at-home was going to thwart his gift of giving - especially for those of us "grandkids" who'd been born later in the year and he'd no longer be on Earth for. So, a few days before he slipped away he handed out to each one of us a sacred birthday card with solid instructions on how "it was only to be opened upon the arrival of our special day." Meanwhile, after once dying peacefully at home only a few days later, this card was quite a comfort – as I now soothingly stashed it under my tear-soaked pillow upon which my snuggled ragdoll, Susie, and I now slept. Furthermore, as my birthday in November seemed so far off into my future, my thoughts of such thankful memories were replaced by the painful reality of losing Poppy's lifelong presence. Though, while dealing with this exact scenario regularly at my E.R. job I was quickly reminded too, that wallowing amidst raw grief is much tougher when it makes an unwelcome appearance upon our own agenda. Now, as these totally forlorn feelings found their place truly right front-and-center, it fatefully occurred to me to take "some really sorry-looking specimens" from Poppy's once-really robust rosebushes and then tenderly next plant them into my three, tiny gardens. And, while unsure of just what color each of them would harbor, it was my intent to breathe new life into them the same way he had done with me. Foremost, I held out hope that these seemingly poor plants would prosper, once comfortably wrapped like I was, amid the welcoming sweetness of spiritual comfort and calm.

Before I knew it November had arrived, bringing with it both my thirty-seventh birthday and Daylight Savings Time, amongst a monsoon of mixed feelings for me. Therefore, those that loved me had suggested I should save opening that so special card left behind by my late grandfather, until bravely completing a Saturday work shift. Yet, strong-willed as I am, I chose to explore this obvious legacy of love first thing in the morning. Remarkably next, as I tore open my "most grateful greeting ever" I found that my precious Poppy had once again remembered me with a rose! You see, perfectly perched on the front of this card was a never-before-seen Gemini rose to help ease the pain of my first birthday without him. While softly appearing in sun-streaked shades of coral pink and creamy peach with bold bursts of fuchsia framing each petal's edge – I suddenly remember Poppy saying, how these beauties were one of his favorites (while also pricelessly being named "The 2000 Rose of the Year" in the same year of his passing.) Then, as I finished getting ready for work that morning my tears flowed freely, a mix of gratefulness and grief from the little girl who truly missed her grandpa. Here too, since Poppy had always ingrained in me to be punctual for my paycheck, I tenderly placed that card in my purse, timely put on my make-up and threw on my coat. When next, as I scurried down my three porch steps on this crisp winter morning and darkness was turning ever slowly to daylight, I could not believe my eyes! Where remarkably blooming beautifully, was one of Poppy's previously rescued rosebushes – and bearing a real Gemini rose for me to savor amid my frost-filled garden as the sun began to blissfully shine. As once again I was able to count on my Grandfather's blessed wisdom to miraculously know just what I needed to make my birthday not only beautiful but bearable. After all, I knew, he must've teamed up with God "to shockingly surprise me twice today" amongst reaching out with heaven-sent roses and always keeping his promises. Amazingly too, while eternally admiring my love for the romantic, Poppy would also send his unexpectedly single again Scorpio granddaughter a guided message that I'd understand - by simply bestowing upon me his blooming gift of blushing, twin Gemini roses. Positively here, I became doubly-blessed that day - as one bud lingered everlasting on the front of my card to surely nestle away, while the other lusciously existed in my own backyard so I would never forget to pray! And, although that God-gifted rosebush never did blossom again, it certainly confirmed for me that: "Even when the lifespan of something I adore seems far too short, the luster of its legacy will continue to live on." Besides, while reaping these rewards that morning amidst a spiritual mix of shock and success, the first-grader in me was rapidly enlightened that we are never too old to enjoy birthday parties – while also uncovering a wonderful reason for being born in the month of November! Moreover, since my Poppy had taught me well throughout life, that "there is nothing a rose cannot kiss and make better," I took my thankful tears with me and headed off to begin my surely-hard-at-times Emergency Room shift. Though, once at my desk, the true meaning of this birthday's blissful awakening continued to be apparent. Where intuitively also, while mentioning the magnitude of this mystical morning miracle to cherished coworkers and curious visitors alike (who couldn't help but notice my unusual combination of smiles mixed with sometimes makeup-smeared sobs), I wholeheartedly knew, the "Your Birthday

Should Be Beautiful" boomerang had mystically uncovered yet another wonderful way to make my festivities favorable.

Then, almost two years later, a lovely lady reappeared in my office which still vividly recalled my vulnerability as a visitor that morning – and wanted to let me in on a little secret. Where foremost here, she proceeded to let me know that she had never forgotten the sensitivity we shared, surrounding that first birthday's "morning of mourning" without my Poppy's stellar presence! Next, she sweetly stated how she was forever awestruck by my strength as she felt I'd courageously continued to provide compassionate care through my tears and all. Miraculously as well, as this priceless scenario delightfully proved that: "Sometimes the sharing of sorrow does not always result in others dismally 'witnessing our wimpiness' but allows us to wallow amidst our enlightenment, even in times of distress." Since to my surprise, the "Your Birthday Should Be Beautiful" boomerang, had again boldly beckoned me from yet another unique perspective. This time though, amongst the unconditional thoughts of a wonderful woman who welcomed our chance to connect! As she too, had been affected by that never-forgotten Labor Day lecture, by opting to slip into my obviously struggling shoes and now grow from the gift of my guidance.

Therefore today (just like my Poppy), I willfully rely on my own trusty birthday book to keep me on top of each date, though I'm still working hard on the written-out-way-in-advance part. Wondrously too, since the "olden days" and the modern inventions of email, cell phones and cheap card outlets – we are left with no excuse for neglecting those that we truly treasure, Where lastly, as a precursor to finishing these pretty heart-wrenching paragraphs, I was next guided to sift through the truly cherished contents of my lifelong, "Love You" box (including a few now-faded columns of so inspiring Ann Landers). Though, it was here, as I was reading through my magical memorabilia in search of that Gemini Rose card (and have sadly also since lost it) that I encountered an especially "sparkling" greeting, previously gifted as well by my late Poppy. Here, while perfectly shaded in hues of soothing pastels and sun-kissed flowers, the yellowed message contained inside still really rocked my reality – sending huge, unexpected shock waves amid my blessings and blunders right home to my heart and soul!

> "Dear Missy,
> It's not every grandparent who's lucky enough to have a granddaughter as wonderful as you.
> You have been such a joy to me through the years –
> I feel fortunate to have been able to spend so much time with you
> And share so much in your life.
> Watching you grow and change into the person you are today
> Is something I wouldn't have missed for the world ...
> You will always be a bright spot in my days
> And that's why as you celebrate another birthday,
> I'm making a wish that all your hopes and dreams come true
> Because what makes you happy,
> Makes me happy too!
> (Where next he wrote)
> Wishing You Happiness Always
> 
> Lots of Love,
> Poppa"

Meanwhile, as I gently placed this beautiful rose-covered box back to rest upon my dresser, I unexpectedly gazed, into my own sparkling mirror – and was shocked to see my own sacred truth shining brightly back at me! As sweetly I've found, that "although life's trials can be full of lonely times and left-behinds," the fact that we bravely keep on loving, is truly where it's at! Somehow also, it has become less of a priority to cling to my past inadequacies, and more prosperous to my intuitive spirit to celebrate my individuality. Incredibly too, since both God and my grandfather had long forgotten my times of being less than perfect, makes my perspective today less about my implied failures and more about the miracles I'm instilled to manifest! Therefore, it has become my turn to forgive myself freely, for thinking some ugly thoughts – about my basically opted out-father and now so-blessed to have nosey neighbors. Yet, even after figuring this out in my late forties how "Living a life that I love freely, foremost stems from within" – I still found the first-grader in me struggling with one very simple question. At this divine moment, "If I dared to deliver a back-at-ya boomerang spiraling off in the direction of heaven, would my Poppy receive it, as well as understand that his repetitive efforts had finally sunk in?" And, if truth be told, although I may never have all the answers, I'm awesomely assured of three things. First off, I will never again come last in my own life, while pledging forever to "say it as I see it." Second, although my Poppy has moved onward (and upward) to greener pastures, he is eternally my Grandfather who still with God's gifted guidance remains only a prayer away. Lastly, while being totally convinced that there are no coincidences in life – it far from shocks me to have successfully completed this "Your Birthday Should Be Beautiful" so-moving-to-me memoir, on none other than my late Poppy's eighty-third birthday. So, in the end to my precious readers, here's to happiness, healing and having it all – amidst an abundance of faith, forgiveness and ever-following your heart!

*** "Do not look forward to what may happen tomorrow, as the same Everlasting Father who cares for you today, will care for you tomorrow and everyday. Either He will shield you from suffering or He will give you the unfailing strength to bear it. Be at peace then, and put aside all anxious thoughts and imaginations."

St. Francis DeSales

"Only in the darkness can you see the stars."
~ Martin Luther King Jr.

A LAST-MINUTE DEDICATION -

# BECAUSE WE ARE NEVER TOO OLD FOR SURPRISES!

One of the best things I can say about working along with God on these book writing missions, is that I never know how they will end. Especially since, I started out while being told by the Lord to highlight my own "Seven Special Sparklers" – yet, only in the last few weeks have been instructed by His Abundant Glory, how there are actually going to be eight!

You see, to know Jennifer Pitarresi is to love her. Whether publically sharing "cute pictures of her two hounds which she considers to be her children," or airing her gripes outright on anyone's improper use of grammar, or ultimately planning at the helm our once, "high school senior class' fiftieth birthday party" (now almost six months ago) - it seemed that whatever Jennifer put her mind to accomplish she more than did with ease. Furthermore, I've sweetly found that after going years without running into her, we would always seem to pick up right where we left off. Such was the case late last summer, when I unexpectedly bumped into her at the grocery store, where I used to work for almost fourteen years. Where somehow too, between the treasured talk of our monumental birthdays now approaching full-speed at about fifteen months away – I happily learned as well, how she was actually only about two weeks older than I was, and also born on the very same November day as my so lucky-to-have little brother! Though, over time here, we both still giggle over the fact that I never did enlighten her as we talked (to avoid more bouts of heightened sabotage), that I had "just birthed my first, God-guided book." Moreover, this tapestry thread of consciously doing the Lord's work would be the one comfort-quilt-connection to blissfully bring us closer - as we both consistently posted to friends and family lots of passages and much loved prayers. Therefore, even between her flamboyant love of Legal work and my merging with the Medical field, it became clear almost instantly, that we two "hadn't-seen-each-other-in-years sisters" sat the same spiritual side of the fence.

Meanwhile, nothing could've seriously prepared us for the crisis heading next. After all, a close group of our cherished classmates had just celebrated this past July of 2013, our combined fiftieth birthday party, which was awesomely organized by Jennifer's skills. Yet, less than one month later on August 28 of this very same summer, our so-sparkling wonder while home all alone in the shower, would suffer a very serious stroke. So serious, in fact, that her doctors were truly undecided, as her family would next understandably share with worry: "Whether to shrink her head's troublesome clot, or to actually go in and remove it." Here too, she was placed in a medically-induced coma, to keep her ailing body both calm and in a condition conducive to helping her heal. Likewise, it would be here in late September, that the hospital staff was having a hard time allowing her fatigued lungs to be able to breathe on their own, which meant removing her first off of a vent. Finally, while all of this was going on, we classmates cheered her on from the sidelines – even causing me to optimally post with tears streaming down my cheeks to one of Jennifer's favorite online pages: "If our prayers could bring you home tomorrow, you'd be there by today." Furthermore we found, that although some of those within our graduated group made it known how they weren't very thrilled about the milestone of turning fifty – more than anything now we each willfully shifted our focus, hoping our friend would just WAKE UP!

As time marched on, Jennifer actually did by the Grace of God awaken, and had some incredibly surreal stories of inspiration from this spiritual adventure to share! Where first off, she states that, "Although she is unsure of the exact timeframe - whether she was basically on the floor of her shower post-stroke, or being unsuccessfully weaned off of the hospital's ventilator" – that she then, "suddenly encountered both of her late parents and a very special aunt who now made their homes in heaven." Here also, while these three family members would each now have their backs totally to her, it would be only then, that her kind-hearted Father would wondrously turn around. Next, she recalls vividly, her Dad softly saying to her now, amongst such a close-knit group: "You're not coming, Jenny. Your brothers and sisters will take care of you." Meanwhile, since miracles always happen every day to those whose eyes and hearts are truly open, although no white lights or other fanfare appeared, she explicitly returned to this Earth just like she had been told. Though, even more amazing as Jennifer continued to tell this tale, was the fact that her repeated efforts to be weaned off of the ventilator never worked, until a cherished girlfriend who'd gone to Italy would share one of her greatest gifts. As it's only, by the healing benefits and blessings of some imported Holy Water being so lovingly placed upon her forehead by her older sister one day - that has allowed an always-faith-first Jennifer, to both excitedly open her eyes and then over-breathe the vent! Where remarkably too, as us aging cheerleaders continue to watch in sheer awe amidst her tiresome days of such really grueling rehab, Jennifer foremost now smiles and takes much less for granted - amidst truly knowing that God's totally got her covered regardless of what happens next. Especially since, it's "only because she reacted so quickly" she says proudly (as I too, have been relentlessly taught also in the E.R.), to this potential stroke case scenario, that she's so gracefully lived-to-tell about both the real blessings of turning fifty amid religiously rebuilding her life.

> "Create the kind of self that you would be happy to live with all your life. Make the most of yourself by fanning the tiny, inner sparks of possibility into flames of achievement."
> ~ Golda Meir

HAPPY 50ᵀᴴ BIRTHDAY JENNIFER PITARRESI -
HERE'S TO SOME MAJORLY BLESSED MIRACLES,
AND ALSO TO REACHING YOUR MOMENT!

"People are like stained-glass windows. They sparkle and shine when the sun is out, but when the darkness sets in, their true beauty is revealed only if there is a light from within."

                    Elisabeth Kubler-Ross

# ABOUT THE AUTHOR

Nancy Loss lives in the Western New York area and remains truly grateful for the God-given ability to light up people's lives. Where foremost today, by willfully learning to become less busy, she continues to walk by both His grace and favor - and is eternally thankful also, for those special friends and family who'll always have her back. Moreover, once stumbling upon the cherished concept herself, of "what it truly means to S.P.A.R.K.L.E." - Nancy aims most to inspire others to pursue this trek as well. Excitedly too, while this second book's journey would again reflect the wondrous bliss behind the Lord's' abundant blessings, she hopes that every reader will also learn to forgive, their own "not-so-sparkling moments," amidst settling now for nothing less, than a stellar life that's meant to be lived! Meanwhile, as it has since been Nancy's biggest challenge to have her book's rough draft submitted in about ninety days to coincide with her fiftieth birthday, she remains totally thrilled that for as much as some others tried to sabotage her creative energy (and even amid some last minute illness to her computer team), she was surreally able to pull this task off!

Yet, in closing she credits most God's light for expediting her manuscript's completion, joyfully combining some real-life heroes' and heroines' courage with the magnificence of His vibrant verses. While spiritually hoping also, that her victorious attempt to "share other's sparkling stories" will appear in print just in time for Valentine's Day, Nancy knows it will only ultimately publish, whenever the Lord sees fit. Where sweetly too, regardless of all the heightened strife and struggles endured, especially within the homestretch - it really is the perfect gift for those who refuse to give up as Nancy also believes, in the refreshing luster of the sand, the sun and the sparkle of living happily ever after!

AND NOW,

## FOR THE REAL ICING ON THE CAKE...

"If we really believe that God is in complete control of our life, none of the things that go wrong will upset or discourage us, because we know that through it all God is working out *His* plan for us. We will not glory in what *we* are doing for God, but only in what He is doing through us.

We must learn to commit our lives to God, trusting ourselves to Him in everything and for everything, relying not upon our great faith but upon His marvelous grace. It is true that faith is important, but even faith comes to us by grace, as a gift. Everything in our lives depends not on our merits or abilities or works but upon God's divine willingness to use His infinite power to meet our needs – and at no cost to us whatsoever.

That is grace."

~ Joyce Meyer

\*\*\* The above quote was taken from, IF NOT FOR THE GRACE OF GOD by Joyce Meyer. Used by permission of Faith Words.

# THE BEST IS YET TO COME!

> "Be strong and of good courage, do not fear nor be afraid of them; for the Lord your God, He is the One who goes with you. He will not leave you nor forsake you."
>
> Deuteronomy 31: 6
> "NKJV™"

Finally, if there's one thing that I've learned, from the last nine months of birthing this book S.P.A.R.K.L.E. – from a once in-my-mind vision to next almost in book format, is that I'm responsible for my own choices. After all, the blinding truth has made it clear (almost in neon lights!) – "How it's totally impossible to fulfill God's will of fruitfully enhancing His Kingdom," if we ultimately stay focused upon what others say we're not. Though, I also owe some thanks here, to those always-negative people who now surely need new hobbies – since I never would have so passionately survived the uphill, of producing some of my best work!

Meanwhile, as my manuscript now progresses to the layout stage, I would like to share a repetitive thought with you. It's one that seemingly has had no problem both moving into the forefront of my cherished happenings by day, yet also keeps consistently waking me up at night - to now humbly add last-minute, this heartfelt wording here. Where at this point, it has been suggested spiritually right to my soul, to "ask anyone who reads this book sacredly full of faith and promise, to refer four more friends to purchase" - as not so much to obtain my once-primary goal of having a New York Times bestseller, but like anyone who has ever played "pass the baton" in gym class - to help propel the Lord's Greatness along.

Here too, I would like to share that God still is answering my prayers today, even more incredibly in ways I understand.

Furthermore, it was during the completion of my "About the Author" section, from my *Life Is How You Look At It,* that I mentioned "how much I was looking forward to becoming a grandmother down the road." Miraculously too, while my first book's final revision date was none other than September 6, 2012 (as listed right inside on the Copyright page), I'm truly over the moon to inform you that my very first grandchild is expected to arrive excitedly this September, on exactly two years from that date! And, while there is no better feeling as a parent, then to watch our children grow to both happily walk down the aisle, and blissfully harbor our grandkids, I now know one more amazing thing for sure. You see, even amidst divinely completing this faith-filled journey, we had such a chilly, icy winter, that our "always-flowing Niagara Falls' water" mixed with Mother Nature's input - did actually freeze over. Therefore, I can still hear both Dr. Torres' trademark, (and foremost married) chuckle amid my special stepmom Lucy, telling me to really be more careful for the stuff that I might wish!

Though in closing, while running a bunch of errands yesterday, although really needing to be parked at my computer, finishing up this ending, I next stopped only to crash my diet before our scheduled "date night" and pick up some Chinese food. But, it wasn't until I got home, that I discovered that my very sweet friend who also owns the restaurant, had snuck in two fortune cookies - and when I so-childishly opened mine up it said: "The best is yet to come." Where, in the end, while this uplifting sentiment gives me, a serious case of the "warm-fuzzies,"- I now gratefully see too, that my mission to vessel my now Eight Exquisite Angel's stories, amongst some other's boldly-asked-for inspiration, was really beyond worth it. Moreover, through all the hefty storms of heightened sabotage amid being left home at times like leftovers - I could *always* feel Christ's faithful presence lovingly holding my hand. Since, it was also my own reflection in the mirror during young, Michael Torres' story, amongst God's unfailing support of "You CAN do this, Missy!" that has kept my destined callings ultimately alive. Yes, the ones to both "reach out and spread more love in this world" while ever-full of a million questions, and then, by willfully becoming a (labeled-by-some) "serious misfit," turned optimally "believable beacon" – who's successfully now leading others to seek His Nurturing Light. Likewise, from reviewing this treasured book's page of sixty-six, awesomely appears, my own most illuminating answer to learning to like my loneliness. Remarkably too, while intuitively knowing also, that this endeavor wouldn't be easy - are the wondrously comforting words: "Sometimes when we don't see it, someone we love, stays right by our side." So in the end, may your life as well, continue to overflow with such an abundance of blessings – that the only way you can explain them, is to never surrender your need to S.P.A.R.K.L.E., and amidst always carrying a working flashlight (in sweet memory of my Poppy) surely credit the Lord's love above!

In peace and prayers …
Love,
Nancy

"Maybe the reason nothing seems to be 'fixing you' is because you're not broken. Let today be the day you stop living within the confines of how others define or judge you. You have a unique beauty and purpose; live accordingly."

~ Dr. Steve Maraboli

# SUGGESTED READING FOR "REAL SPARKLERS"

*The Joy Diet – 10 Daily Practices For A Happier Life* by Martha Beck
*The 5 Love Languages* by Gary Chapman

Any of the books below by Barbara D'Angelis:
*Are You the One For Me?*
*Passion*
*Real Moments®*
*and lastly,*
*Secrets About Life Every Woman Should Know*

*Light in My Darkness* by Helen Keller
*Without a Word How a Boy's Unspoken Love Changed Everything* by Jill Kelly
*The Best of Ann Landers Her Favorite Letters of All Time* by Ann Landers
*In Pursuit of Peace* by Joyce Meyer
*If Not For The Grace Of God* by Joyce Meyer
*Seven Things That Steal Your Joy* by Joyce Meyer
*Become a Better You* by Joel Osteen
*The Body Reset Diet* by Harley Pasternak, M.Sc.
*5-Factor Fitness* by Harley Pasternak, M.Sc. with Ethan Boldt
*Angels 101* by Doreen Virtue, Ph.D.
Finally, *Divine Guidance How To Have a Dialogue with God And Your Guardian Angels,* also by Doreen Virtue, Ph.D.

CPSIA information can be obtained at www.ICGtesting.com
Printed in the USA
BVOW03*1458280514

354456BV00009B/75/P